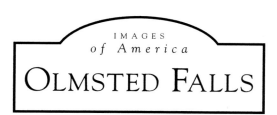

IMAGES
of America

OLMSTED FALLS

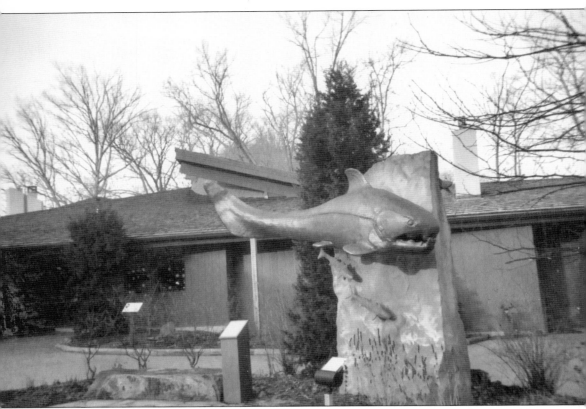

Prehistoric times and the early history of this area can be studied at the Rocky River Nature Center located at Shephard Lane and Valley Parkway in Cleveland Metroparks. Rocky River Reservation extends through eight communities and encompasses 2,552 acres. Cleveland Metroparks was established in 1917 to preserve the natural valleys of the area and to provide open spaces for the people of Greater Cleveland and visitors to enjoy.

On the cover: Olmsted Falls City Hall and police headquarters and government offices are seen here. The building dates back to 1916 when it was built as the central school of the community. Its use as a high school ended in 1968. It continued as a middle school until 1996. The photograph is of the last class in this building on the last day of school before summer vacation. The students look anxious to begin their summer fun. It is the largest and most impressive public building of Olmsted Falls. (Cleveland State University, Cleveland Press Collection.)

IMAGES
of America

OLMSTED FALLS

John D. Cimperman

ARCADIA
PUBLISHING

Published by Arcadia Publishing
Charleston SC, Chicago IL, Portsmouth NH, San Francisco CA

Printed in the United States of America

Library of Congress Catalog Card Number: 2007926858

For all general information contact Arcadia Publishing at:
Telephone 843-853-2070
Fax 843-853-0044
E-mail sales@arcadiapublishing.com
For customer service and orders:
Toll-Free 1-888-313-2665

Visit us on the Internet at www.arcadiapublishing.com

To Julie, my beloved daughter, who is dearly missed.
She was a gifted artist who loved Olmsted Falls.

CONTENTS

ACKNOWLEDGMENTS

Material for this book has been gathered from many sources, and I hope I do not forget to thank all those who provided information, photographs, or their special collections. Throughout the book I will try to identify the individual, organization, and source of all material rather than in the acknowledgments.

But I am greatly indebted to the following for their courtesies and help: Joseph Cimperman, Janice Petrick, Clint Williams, Bill Nickels, Jan Valore, Bev Smith, Ralph Jock, Marilyn Quay Sparks, Steve McQuillin, Robert Lamb, Dale Thomas, Gail Rapps of Northrop Books, Jason Werner, Robert Venefra, Jim and Joyce Boddy, Bruce and Jean Johnson, Michelle Neudeck, Beverly Weseling, Deborah Pabetz, the Ohio Historical Society, the Early Settlers Association of the Western Reserve, the Western Reserve Historical Society, the Historical Society of Olmsted Falls, Frostville Museum, Cleveland Public Library History and Geography Department, North Olmsted Historical Society, Connecticut State Library, and many others who provided material for the book.

INTRODUCTION

The story of Olmsted Falls begins with the story of Connecticut's Western Reserve. It is a history that is an important part of the early history of the United States. It all began in 1662, when King Charles II of England granted Connecticut all lands bounded by the colony from sea to sea. It was said that Charles had a greater knowledge of liqueur than geography. The king did not know how much land he was giving, and Connecticut did not know what it was getting. Remember this was before the Lewis and Clark age of discovery. When our new government was formed, Connecticut relinquished all of its western lands to the federal government, except for the land that it called the Western Reserve, or New Connecticut. The Northwest Territory was established in 1787, and the claims of the colonies had to be settled. Massachusetts, New York, and Virginia had claims granted by English kings. All gave up their claims to the new government except for Connecticut, which retained its Western Reserve. Connecticut set aside about 500,000 acres of the reserve for the benefit of citizens who had suffered losses by fire during the Revolution; it called the land the "Fire Lands." During the Revolution, British troops would burn the property of people suspected of supporting the American cause. The Fire Lands would be today's Erie and Huron Counties.

Let us step back even further in time to the prehistoric period. Following the departure of the glaciers, the first humans to enter the region did so as early as 12,000 to 10,000 B.C. They were small hunting groups following the mastodon and mammoth. Many migrating hunting tribes entered the region. One of those tribes, the Erie, gained control of the southern shore of the lake from Sandusky Bay to today's Buffalo. At the time of the discovery of the Eries by the French Jesuit missionaries, the Cuyahoga River, the Rocky River, and the Portage Lakes seemed to be an important region for the Eries. The area was rich in wildlife, fish, and berries for the picking, and the soil was rich for growing. Unfortunately for the Eries, their control of the region was not to last; the Iroquois became their bitter enemies. The Iroquois, who lived in what is today Quebec, Ontario, and New York State, joined with other tribes to form the Six Nations. In the middle of the 17th century, the Iroquois with their allies defeated the Eries and took control of what is today northeast Ohio. Moses Cleaveland was chosen by the Connecticut Land Company to lead a surveying party to meet with the Native Americans and negotiate the sale of the western lands. He served under George Washington as a general during the Revolutionary War and rose to the rank of brigadier general in the Connecticut Militia. It was the Six Nations of the Iroquois that General Cleaveland met with to negotiate the sale of the western lands. A Mohawk chief named Joseph Brant served as a spokesman for his people. He was a Christian missionary of the Anglican Church and a British military officer. Brant was born in 1742 on the banks of the

Ohio River and given the Native American name Thayendanegea. The name Thayendanegea means "he who places two bets." He did not place two bets but stayed loyal to the crown and was rewarded for his loyalty. After the war, he received a land grant of 675,000 acres in Canada for Mohawk losses during the Revolutionary War. Brant died on August 24, 1807, in Canada and Moses Cleaveland at his home in Connecticut in 1806. Both men lived long enough that they may have been informed of the second sale of the lands of the Western Reserve at the Treaty of Fort Industry in 1805, when the Native American tribes west of the Cuyahoga River sold the western lands of the reserve to the Connecticut Land Company.

If there is anything you remember from this book, I hope it is the courage and determination of those early settlers to make their life meaningful. I read the following on a flyer, so I do not know who to attribute it to, but I believe it is profound and best identifies all those who came to America and the Western Reserve in those early days when this land was a wilderness. The flyer read, "I dare you to sacrifice a life pre-determined with guided direction and ease for a path of unknown challenges and choice—bestowed the freedom to fail and grow—thus experiencing the gift of life." I do not know how it could be said in any better way.

One

THE MOVE WESTWARD

Congress ratified the Declaration of Independence by the 13 colonies on July 4, 1776. This was the first step to develop the United States as it is known today. Then came the Revolutionary War. That war continued for seven years until 1783, when a peace treaty was signed. But that did not end the conflict. It was thought that Britain had relinquished all of Ohio to the United States. That was not the case; British activity did not conclude until after the War of 1812 and Oliver Hazard Perry's victory in the Battle of Lake Erie. That battle essentially established the northern boundary of the United States. After Perry's victory, Gen. William Henry Harrison pursued the fleeing British and Native Americans into Canada and fought the Battle of Thames on October 5, 1813. In December 1814, at what was called the Treaty of Ghent, it was established that the Great Lakes, not the Ohio River, would be the northern boundary between the United States and Canada.

A trip to Put-in-Bay, the Perry Monument, and the new education center tells the story of that momentous time in American history. One may want to start a tour of history at the Western Reserve Historical Society located in Cleveland's renowned arts and culture center called University Circle. The mission of the society is to collect, preserve, and present the history of all the people of the Western Reserve.

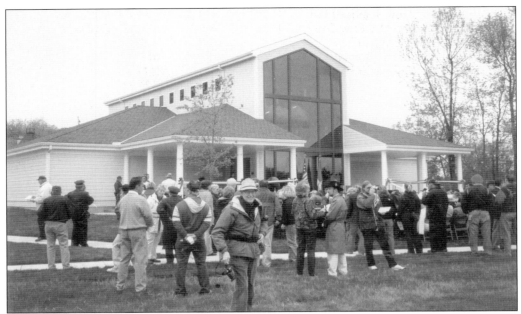

Dedication of the $2.5 million education center at Put-in-Bay was celebrated on May 18, 2002. The center vividly tells the story of Oliver Hazard Perry's victory on September 10, 1813, that secured control of Lake Erie for the United States and the lasting peace that was established between the United States, Great Britain, and Canada. The man facing the camera is Gil True, officer of the Early Settlers Association of the Western Reserve.

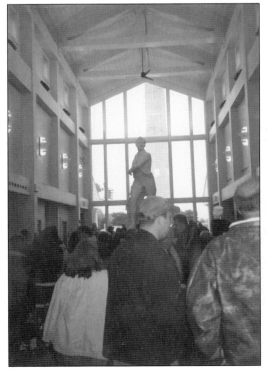

From the interior of the education center, the Perry Monument can be seen and through the window, the 352-foot Perry Doric Column. The Perry statue originally stood on Cleveland Public Square in 1860. It was replaced in 1929 with a bronze statue that now stands in Fort Huntington Park in Cleveland. The original statue is preserved from the weather at its new location in the education center at Put-in-Bay.

The Perry Doric column stands 47 feet taller than the Statue of Liberty. The observation gallery located 317 feet above Lake Erie offers a panoramic view of Put-in-Bay and the Lake Erie Islands.

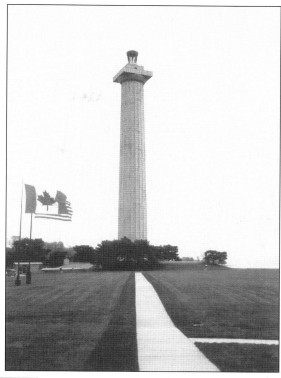

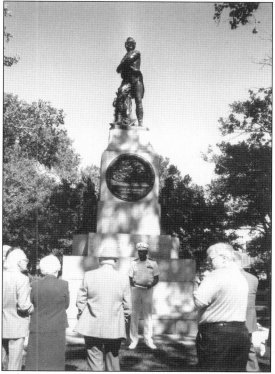

Annually on September 10, the anniversary of the Battle of Lake Erie, the Early Settlers Association of the Western Reserve conducts a program at Fort Huntington Park located at East Sixth Street and Lakeside Avenue in downtown Cleveland to commemorate Perry's victory. Fort Huntington was a War of 1812 fort. Historic markers at the park tell the story of that momentous time in history.

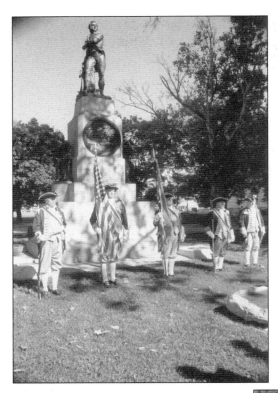

The Western Reserve chapter of the Sons of the American Revolution Color Guard join with the Early Settlers Association each year in the program at the site of the Perry Monument in Cleveland. Seen here are, from left to right, Robert Shepard, Lafayette chapter of the Sons of the American Revolution; John Franklin; Frances Sherman; Hugh Harris; and Ruluff McIntyre of the Western Reserve Society Sons of the American Revolution. (Gil True.)

This photograph, taken at a City of Cleveland birthday that was celebrated on July 22, 2003, is that of the Moses Cleaveland statue that stands on Cleveland Public Square. Photographed from left to right are John Franklin, color guard attached to the Western Reserve chapter of the Sons of the American Revolution; Cleveland city councilman Joseph Cimperman; Mary Bacon Artino, a descendant of Moses Cleaveland, and her son Michael; and Dr. Robert E. Bartholomew.

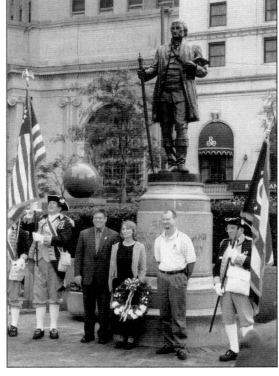

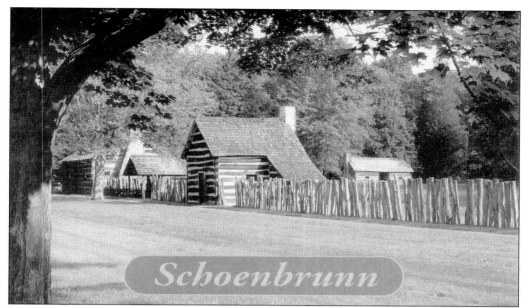

Schoenbrunn

To further study and understand life in those early days, one should plan a visit to Hale Homestead near Bath and to Schoenbrunn Village in New Philadelphia. The visit is well worth the trip. Beginning as early as 1761, the Moravian Brethren, a German Protestant sect, worked to Christianize the Native Americans. By 1772, a mission was established along the Tuscarawas River called Schoenbrunn.

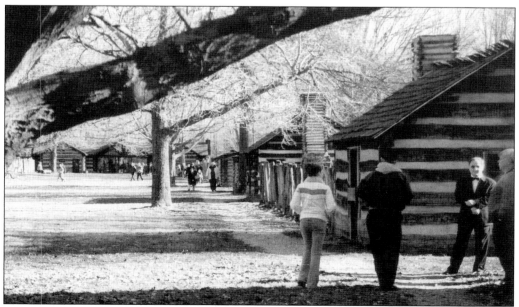

Today's reconstructed Schoenbrunn Village consists of 17 log structures, two acres of planted fields, and the original cemetery. *Schoenbrunn* is the German word for "beautiful spring." A museum offers information on life in the village. The visit also gives one an understanding of how life and shelter existed for the early settlers throughout Ohio, including Olmsted Falls, in those early days.

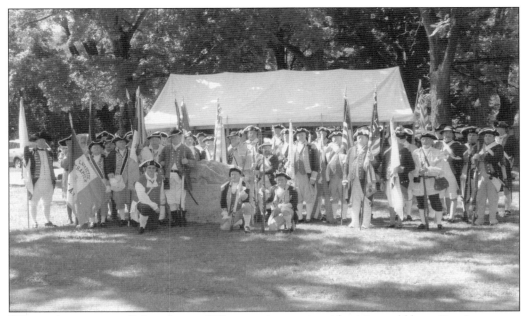

When taking a trip to Schoenbrunn Village, an interesting side visit would be to Fort Laurens, a 1778 fort located on the banks of the Tuscarawas River near Bolivar. Fort Laurens is Ohio's only Revolutionary War fort. Fort Laurens's museum details the history of the military campaign and includes items unearthed at the site. Each year, the Sons of the American Revolution chapters from Ohio and nearby states gather at Fort Laurens. (John Franklin collection.)

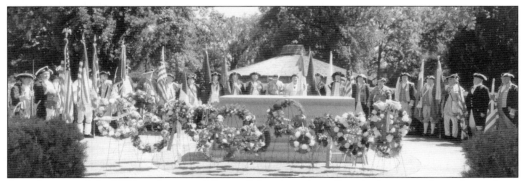

Seen here is a July 2003 gathering of Sons of the American Revolution units from throughout the state of Ohio and nearby states at Fort Laurens. Only a short distance from Fort Laurens is Zoar Village State Memorial. Zoar Village was founded in the fall of 1817 by a group of about 200 German separatists who were seeking to escape religious persecution in their homeland. Today it is preserved by the Ohio Historical Society as a state memorial.

Two

FROSTVILLE

Just a short distance from the nature center at Valley Parkway and Cedar Point Road is Frostville Museum, an affiliate of Cleveland Metroparks. There one can experience life as it was lived by those early settlers of the Rocky River valley. Frostville is managed by the Olmsted Historical Society, a nonprofit association of visionary volunteers. It receives no revenue from tax dollars, yet it has been able to continue to add buildings and improve its historical collections.

Frostville is named after Elias C. Frost's post office, opened in 1829. His farm was located at what is today the intersection of Kennedy Ridge, Columbia, and Mastick Roads. Cedar Point Road was surveyed and made a county road in the 1820s. Cedar Point and the Cedar Valley received their names from the group of cedar trees that grew on the high bluff where the east and west branches of the Rocky River meet. The story of Cedar Valley is an important part of the history of the area. The wilderness that became Olmsted Falls began to change when the Connecticut Land Company offered for sale its land called the Western Reserve, or New Connecticut. For those early settlers, the journey to the western lands was extremely hazardous through the uncharted wilderness to build a new life in a new land. Frostville Museum provides the visitor with an opportunity to see and feel life as it was in those early days. Through the work of the Olmsted Historical Society, its members, and its friends, history is brought back to life, surrounded by preserved buildings that played a part in forming its history.

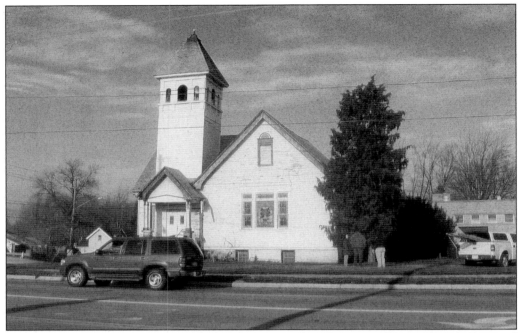

Pictured is the historic Barton Road Church as it stood on Barton and Lorain Roads. It served many congregations over the years, and today there are still many mysteries about the church history. (Frostville Museum collection.)

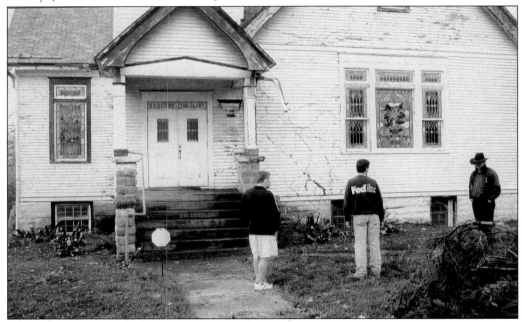

The committee is seen here considering its move of the Barton Road Church to Frostville. The man in the middle, wearing a FedEx shirt, is Robert Lamb, who is a member of the Olmsted Historical Society. He was active in the development of the Frostville Museum and is a man who was very helpful in the writing of this book. (Frostville Museum collection.)

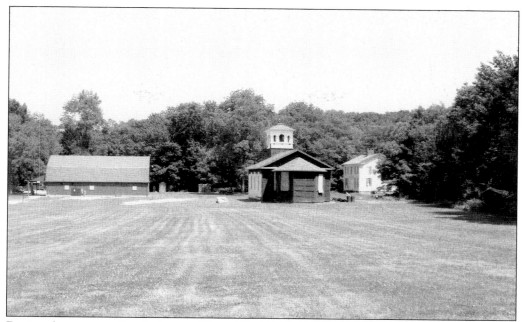

During the summer, Revolutionary War to World War II encampments are held on the green of Frostville. Looking across the very peaceful green, one can see both the display barn that was built in 1976 as a bicentennial project and the Barton Road Church, which is under restoration. (Dale Thomas collection.)

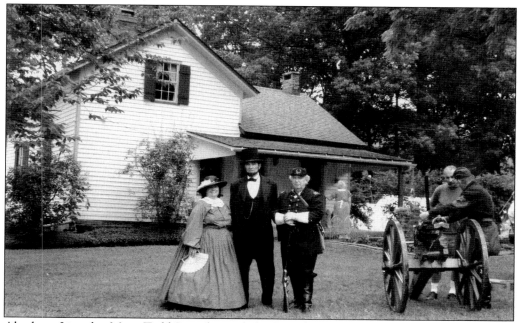

Abraham Lincoln, Mary Todd Lincoln, and the Lincoln guard impersonators are in front of the Prechtel House, the only building that remained on its original site in the village that at one time included 13 homes of the small rural community of the Cedar Valley. (Dale Thomas collection.)

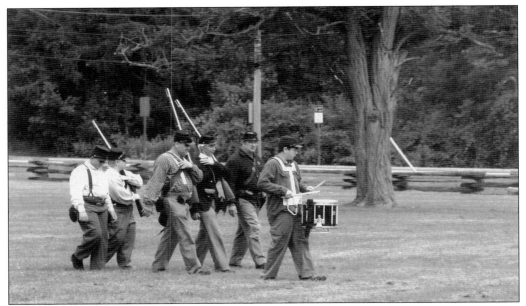

Members of the 7th Ohio Volunteer Infantry and United States Sharp Shooters Company C, 2nd Regiment, pose in full uniform. During the Civil War, it was said that one could not find an able-bodied man in Olmsted who was not in a Union uniform. At the cemeteries in and around Olmsted Falls, especially Butternut Ridge, soldiers' headstones from the Revolutionary War, Civil War, and other engagements of the United States can be found. (Frostville Museum collection.)

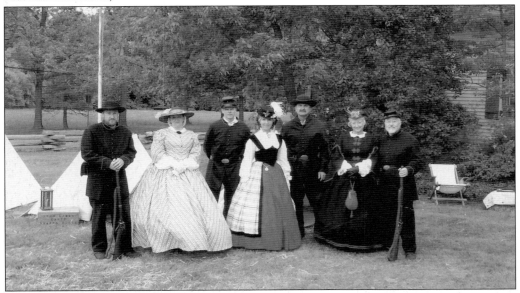

The Civil War remains the nation's central national epic. Americans should not hope to understand themselves or their nation without coming to understand the war that changed the union of states in the United States of America. Through encampments, there is an opportunity to teach children the sacrifices of those early Americans, who by their deprivation and bravery formed the United States that exists today. (Frostville Museum collection.)

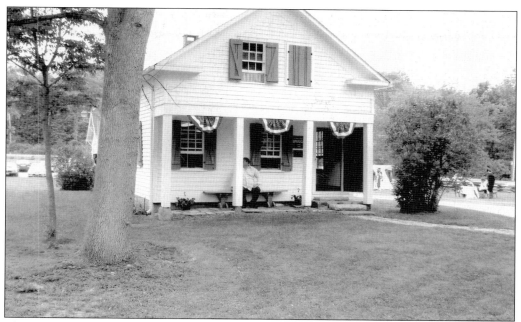

The Briggs House (built about 1836) is also at Frostville. It is today a museum primarily with exhibits from the wars of the nation. The wars had a grave effect on Olmsted Falls, as they did on the nation. It is important that their sacrifice is remembered. Also in the Briggs House, pictures of pioneer families and their descendants are featured throughout the building. The Briggs family arrived in the early 1800s. Thomas Briggs hired John Ames, who came to the Olmsted area in 1834 and built a new home to replace the cabin. Ames used the Greek Revival style popular at the time. The Briggs House remained in the family for over 130 years. It was given to the Olmsted Historical Society and moved to Frostville in 1969.

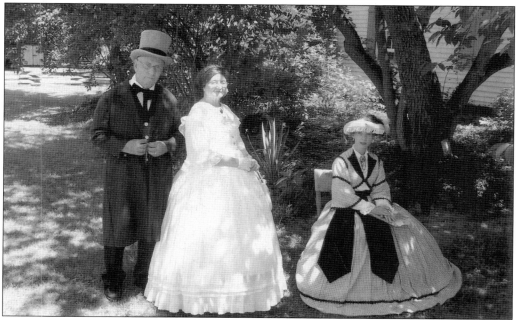

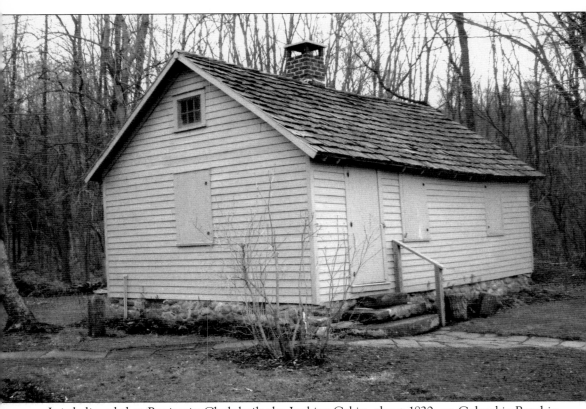

It is believed that Benjamin Clark built the Jenkins Cabin, about 1820, on Columbia Road in what is today North Olmsted near the Westlake border. Sugar (Coe) Ridge was an unbroken wilderness at the time, except for the land around the Clark Cabin. He was a squatter on land owned by Asher M. Coe, who still was living in Connecticut. In 1823, Coe came to the Western Reserve and evicted Clark and moved into the house. He then built a more substantial residence. He later used the Clark Cabin for his farmworkers. The ownership changed a number of times; after undergoing many changes, including two additions, the cabin remained in the ownership of the Jenkins family for over 120 years. In the spring of 1976, Esther Peitrick, a Jenkins descendant, donated the cabin to the Olmsted Historical Society. After the move to Frostville, it was restored and opened in 1980. In the cabin one will see an extensive collection of early settler and Native American artifacts.

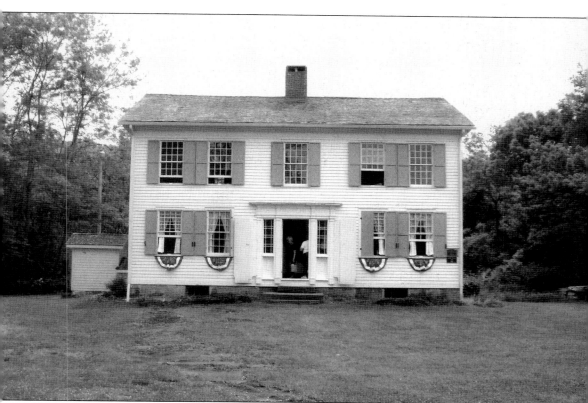

John Carpenter (1786–1861), who worked as a carpenter and farmer, brought his family to Ohio about 1828. The Carpenter House (built about 1831) is identified as the earliest remaining Federal-style home in North Olmsted. One of the sons of John Carpenter, William (1813–1877), was at one time the owner of the Grand Pacific Hotel that he called De-Carpenter Hotel. According to Beverly Weseling, who did extensive research on the history of the house, the Carpenter House remained in the family until foreclosure in 1940. The home was purchased six years later by the Kitson family, who lived in the house until the early 1980s. Jacqueline Kitson and her husband, Jack Boss, were instrumental in the preservation of the house. Forest Kitson, Jacqueline's father, donated the house to the Olmsted Historical Society; in May 1987, the society moved the building board by board and stone by stone to Frostville. The History Channel's *Civil War Journal* used the house parlor for the 1994 segment on the life of Gen. James A. Longstreet. The interior is mostly furnished with mid-19th-century implements and furnishings.

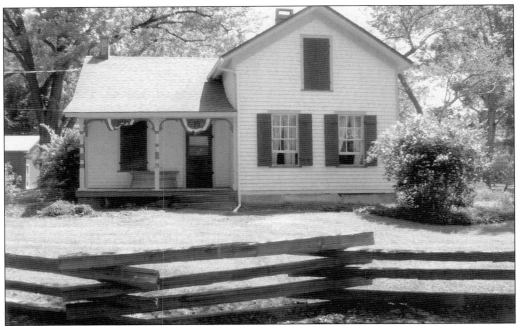

The Prechtel House is the only building original to the property. Built on-site in 1876, it was one of 13 homes in the small community of Cedar Valley, the area that is now Cleveland Metroparks. It was sold to the Cleveland Metropolitan Park Board in 1925, but it continued to be lived in until 1950. In 1962, the board gave permission for the North Olmsted Historical Society to use the building and part of the land as a museum. After making improvements, the society used the house as a meeting place until it opened it as a public museum in 1965. The house has been carefully restored. It is furnished to reflect life in the late American Victorian period.

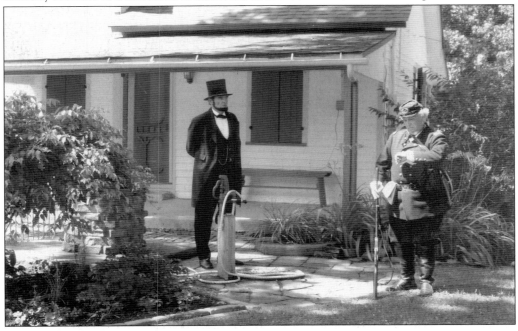

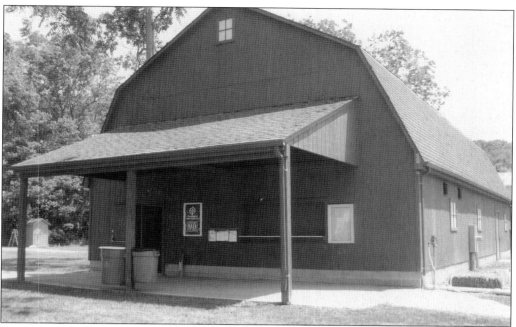

From the first days of the republic, the nation was dependent on the citizen farmers for its stability and its freedom. Barns, as the main structures of farms, evoke a sense of connection with the past. The display barn of Frostville was built as a bicentennial project to display historic items received by the society. Other buildings of Frostville include the Red Barn (pictured here) that is used for special events and is available for private parties. The general store is both a museum with a 19th-century post office and a gift shop. The carriage house was built about 1900 as part of the Stearns farm. Frostville has an archives room that contains genealogical files and other material related to the history of North Olmsted, Olmsted Falls, and Olmsted Township.

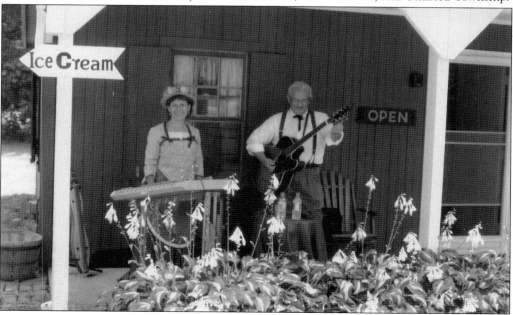

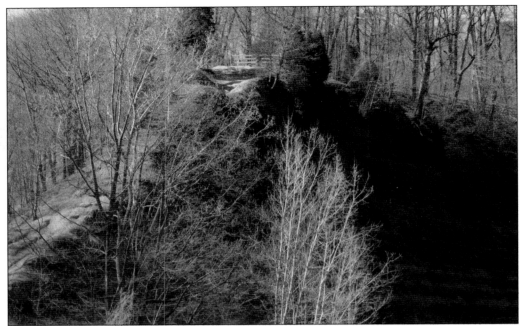

Just across the road from Frostville Museum is Fort Hill and at its base beautiful picnic grounds. From the top is a great view of the valley. At the site there are man-made earth ridges built over 1,200 years ago. The earth ridges built on top of the steep cliffs are thought to have been made for defense. Artifacts found in the area date back to 8000 B.C.

Who was up on Fort Hill?

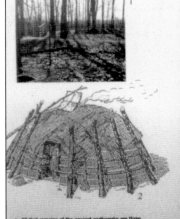

It's a mystery! Much is still unknown about the creation of the Fort Hill earthworks near the nature center. We know people were here long ago—for defense or ritual?

On top of Fort Hill by the nature center, man-made earth ridges were built around 1,200 years ago, so we know people were here many years ago. Over time, farming and erosion have worn down these ridges. Sites with steep cliffs and water, like Fort Hill, are thought to have been chosen for defense. These included wooden post enclosures and wigwam style houses covered with skin, bark or thatch. Without such signs of settlement, archeologists think Fort Hill was a special ceremonial place. Later people, such as the Whittlesey Indians, may have stayed there temporarily for defensive purposes as tensions arose with increasing competition for resources. The true reason for the earthworks remains a mystery.

Visit Fort Hill behind the nature center. What do you think occurred here? Please stay on the trail to avoid further damage.

1 All that remains of the ancient earthworks are three low ridges. Visit Fort Hill for further information.

2 Although, no evidence of settlement has been found

On the trail behind the nature center are steps that will lead to Fort Hill. James Ruple came to the valley in the 1850s and built a house at the foot of Fort Hill. He married, cleared the land, and planted a vineyard atop the hill. The remains of the fort, arrowheads, tomahawks, and other artifacts found in the area tell a story of the battles that must have been fought there.

Three

FROM SETTLEMENT TO CITY

The first settler, James Geer, came to the area when it was called Kingston, named by the surveyors of Connecticut Land Company. Geer was born on January 5, 1778, and came to the Western Reserve in 1807. On January 1, 1808, Geer and Mary Parker received their marriage license. They had a son named Calvin who had the distinction of being the first settler's child born in the Western Reserve. It was said that Geer was an ardent antislavery advocate and served as a link in the Underground Railroad as early as 1820. Other early settlers' names, such as Stearns, Fitch, Cook, and Usher, can be seen on local road signs. As it was said by William Ganson Rose in his book *Cleveland: The Making of a City*, "Despite the many dangers the pioneers sought opportunity at the frontier, ax in one hand, rifle in the other, Bible and spelling book in the saddle bags." They were prepared for a bitter struggle to provide food, clothing, and shelter. It is hoped that the people today, and those who come after who benefit from the sacrifice of those early settlers who braved the wilderness, will remember that it took bravery and hard work to build the cities and towns that make up the states and the nation.

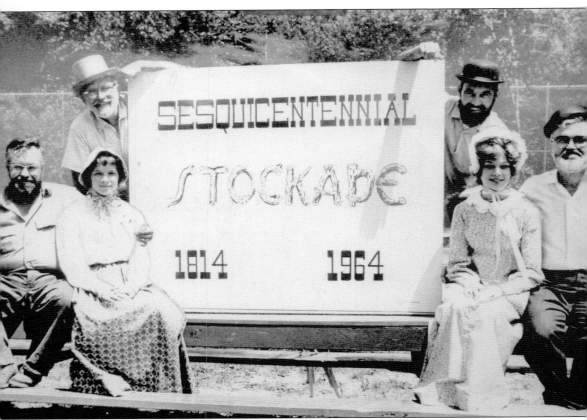

Olmsted Falls was known as township 6, range 15, by the Connecticut Land Company. The surveyors called it Kingston. The community then named it Plum Creek in 1807; then back to Kingston in 1814; in 1823, Lenox; in 1843, Norris Falls. In 1857, Plum Creek and the Village of Olmsted Falls became one community. The name derives from Aaron Olmstead, who bought the acreage of land described as township 6, range 15. He died before he ever saw the land and before his bid was accepted. It was his son Charles who offered to present a library to the community if the town were named Olmstead. The offer was accepted, and the town was called Olmsted. As in the case of Cleaveland, the *a* was dropped. In 1971, the Village of Olmsted Falls and Westview merged, and in 1972, the City of Olmsted Falls was established. Pictured above at the 1964 sesquicentennial celebration are, from left to right, (first row) Ralph Offenberg, Laura Patalon, Kathy Foley, and Steve Lercel; (second row) George Matther and Richard Mellott. (Cleveland State University, Cleveland Press Collection.)

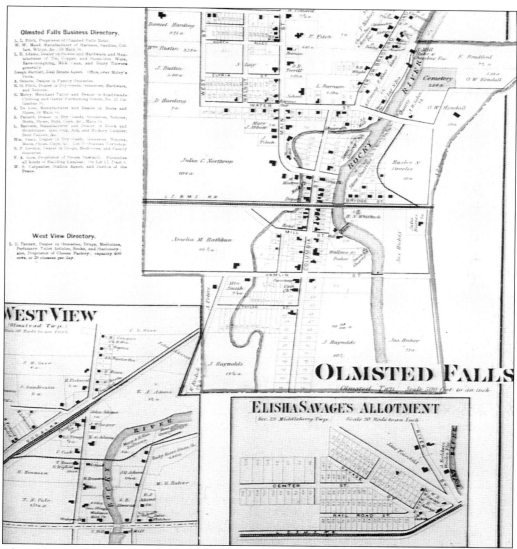

The *Atlas of Cuyahoga County, Ohio* was completed from actual surveys by and under the direction of D. J. Lake, C. E. Lake published the atlas in 1874 in Philadelphia with Titus, Simmons and Titus. It was one of two such commercial atlases of Cleveland to appear in 1874. It is highly detailed and has become a staple for local history and genealogical research into 19th-century Cuyahoga County. The Cleveland State University Library contracted to digitize the maps and illustrations and then reformatted them as LizardTech's DjVu files and mounted them to the Web. The illustrations of private and public buildings were added to the library's image database, and all are freely available through the Web site. It is called the Cuyahoga Historic Atlas Project.

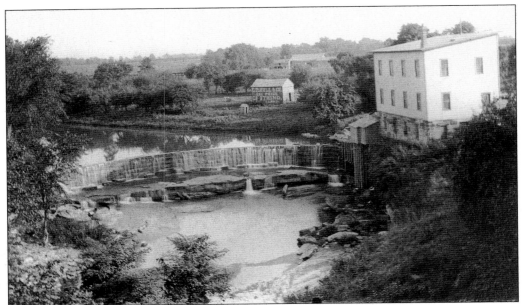

Col. H. N. Whitbeck, a Civil War veteran, built a gristmill on the Rocky River in the 1870s, and he later sold to Ed Damp, who also was a Civil War veteran. Damp built it into one of the most productive mills of the area. In 1883, a flood damaged the mill and the original foundation. A new sandstone foundation and building were constructed at the same location. (Bill Nickels.)

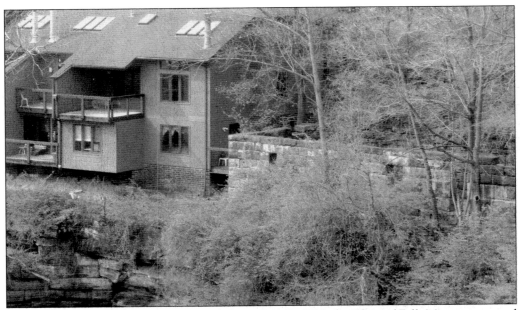

The remains of the mill house stood until about 1943. In 1950, the Olmsted Falls Masons proposed using the foundation for the construction of a Masonic hall at the site. It never happened, but the foundation remains as an Olmsted Falls landmark. The photograph above is of the same location today. To the right are the foundation stones of the old mill, and to the left are the Mill Run Condominiums.

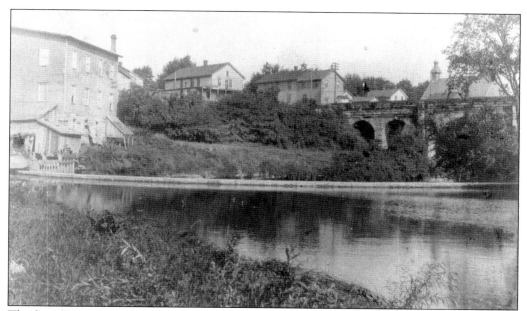

The foundation of the Damp's Flour and Grist Mill can be seen along the river today. There is an observation platform behind Falls Family Restaurant. The restaurant is located at 8079 Columbia Road. In 1883, a flood damaged the mill and foundation. There were more damaging floods to come. In 1913, another flood destroyed most of the mill house leaving only some support beams and the foundation that can be seen today.

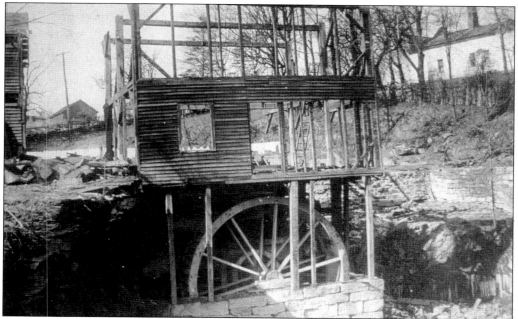

In the 1820s, the first grist- and sawmills were built along the west branch of the Rocky River. The Rocky River and Plum Creek brought those early settlers to what is today Olmsted Falls. They could harness the water flow to operate their gristmills and flour mills. The photograph is of a smaller mill as it fell into disrepair.

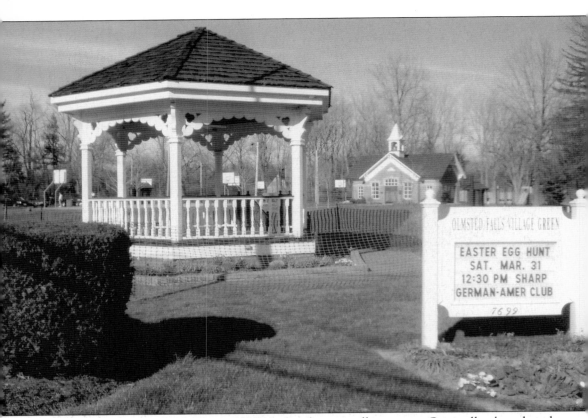

Nothing more represents Olmsted Falls today than its village green. Originally plotted as the public square of the hamlet of Plum Creek, a village that became part of Olmsted Falls in 1857, the village green is located at the corner of Columbia Road and Water Street. Olmsted Falls recognized that there was a time when village bandstands on the green served as gathering places for communities all over America. In 1970, a bandstand was added to the village green. In his book *The Oberlin Book of Bandstands*, S. Frederick Starr describes it this way: "Surviving bandstands with their whimsical gingerbread trim and the music of John Philip Sousa and Charles Ives still recall this phase of American cultural history." That magic can again be experienced during the summer on Olmsted Falls's village green. The brick building seen in the rear of the photograph was built in 2003 to remind people of the schoolhouse that once stood on the site. It acts as a pavilion for the park.

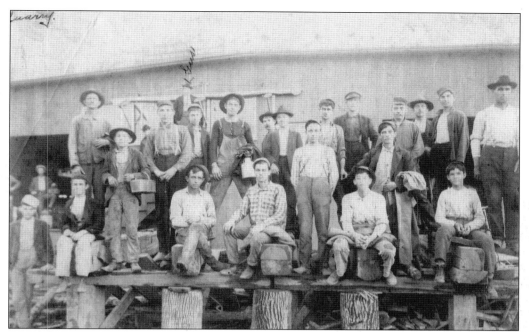

Just a short distance from the village green is Fortier Park, named for David Fortier, a former mayor of Olmsted Falls who died in an automobile accident. As mayor, one of his goals was to improve the parks of Olmsted Falls. The park contains remains of the sandstone quarry, bridges, pavilion, and other improvements completed by the Works Project Administration (WPA). The historic photograph is of the quarry workers taken sometime in the 1870s.

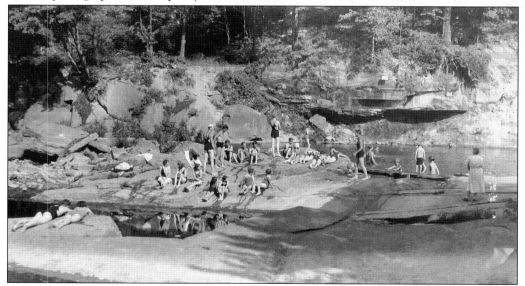

At one time, lifeguards were assigned to protect swimmers on what was called "Slippery Rock" in what is today Fortier Park, where the Rocky River and Plum Creek meet. It does not take a great deal of imagination to understand why it was called Slippery Rock. As one walks along the river and through the park, one will see the remains of the quarry started by Luther Barnum. Blocks of stone used for foundations, sidewalks, and curbstones can also be seen.

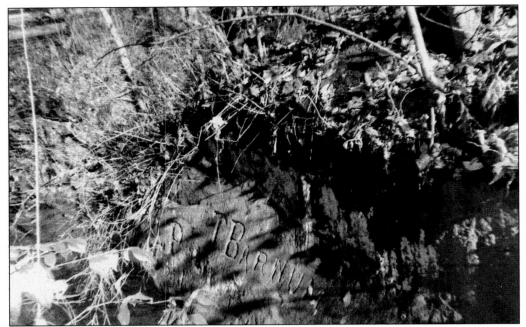

Tom Barnum's carving is pictured here at the location where Plum Creek meets the Rocky River. One can stand in the bridge over Plum Creek in Fortier Park and see the hand-carved name of "T. Barnum." Tom was the grandson of Luther Barnum, who operated the main quarry in Olmsted Falls with his sons Tom and Harry from 1873 to 1876. Luther served as mayor of Olmsted Falls from 1872 to 1875.

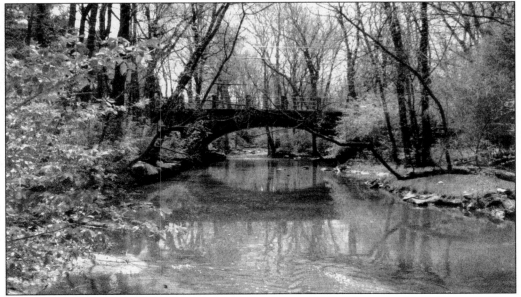

If one follows the Dan Waugh Trail behind the Olmsted Falls Library on Main Street to Plum Creek, one will see the location of the Stokes Mill and the falls that Olmsted Falls is named after. Looking south up the creek one will see what is called Park Drive Bridge over Plum Creek, a stone-faced bridge built as part of the 1930 WPA work project.

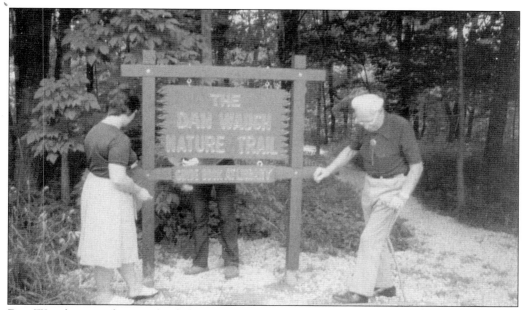

Dan Waugh is seen here at the dedication of the nature trail. The path leads to a platform where Plum Creek Falls (the falls that the town was named after) can be viewed. Some of the remaining foundation stones of the old mill can also be seen, built by Joseph Olmstead Loomis and his son, Newton P. Loomis, in 1844. The Olmsted Falls Library building was the Loomis home.

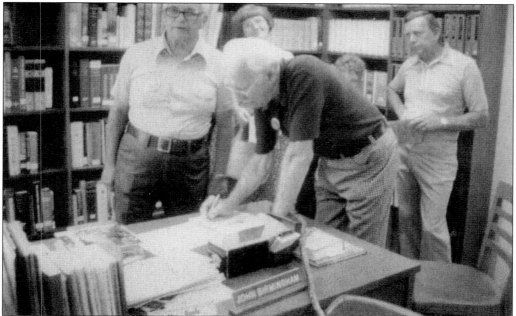

Waugh came to Olmsted Falls in 1925. He served with the New York Calvary, then enlisted in the U.S. Marines in World War I. He returned from duty seriously injured and was told not to expect to walk again. Waugh put his therapy to work for many people to enjoy as a nature columnist for the *Sun Papers*, a northern Ohio weekly publication. His column was called "Nature Rambles." The photograph was taken at a book signing.

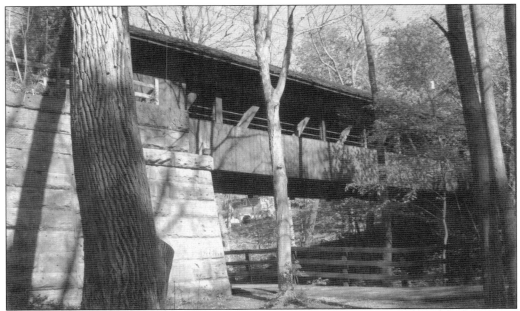

This view shows the covered bridge from Olmsted Falls Village Park. The park trail is a scenic walk along Mill Creek, to where the creek meets the Rocky River. Evidence of the Olmsted Falls quarry that began in operation in 1873 can be seen. Luther Barnum, grandson of early pioneer John Barnum, worked the quarry from 1873 to 1876. The Cleveland Stone Company bought out all the quarries of the area in 1886.

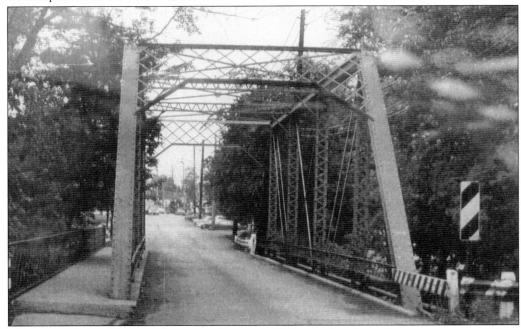

This 1909 iron trestle bridge carried traffic over Mill Creek when Main Street was open to Water Street. The bridge was closed to traffic, and in 1998, the covered wooden pedestrian bridge replaced it and today provides a location for many civic events such as Art on the Bridge.

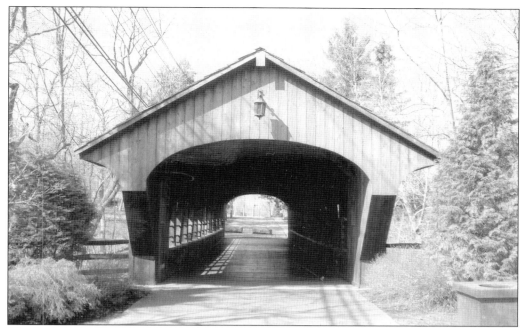

The bridge is named after Capt. Charles A. Harding, a fourth-generation resident of Olmsted Falls who died of wounds received during the Battle of Normandy in the World War II. The road over the bridge is no longer open, but it serves as a great backdrop for photographers. Many wedding parties have been photographed on the Harding Bridge.

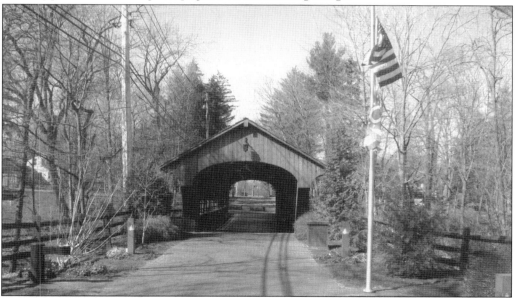

The covered wooden bridge was built as a tribute to Captain Harding by his sisters, Amelia and Clara Harding, and the community. It was a community effort. The Olmsted Falls Kiwanis Club formed a committee to undertake the project. Amelia and Clara provided the initial money to begin the project, and the city and state offered the remaining funds necessary to complete the bridge.

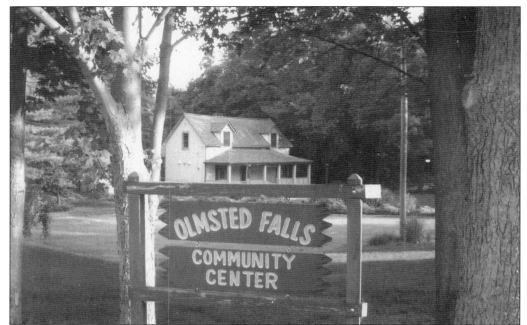

The August Von Brouse blacksmith shop was located at 7932 Main Street. Today it is the Jenkins Community Center. Von Brouse also served as town marshal, as was the case in small towns. The blacksmith had to be a man of significant stature, strong, and tough.

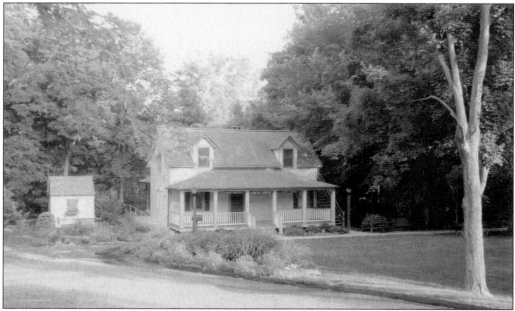

Olmsted Falls's Jenkins Community Center is located at 7932 Main Street and is named for Bill Jenkins, who came to Olmsted Falls in 1935. He served on council for three terms and was clerk for two and a half years. He followed Dan Waugh as scoutmaster and was president of the Kiwanis Club. Walter F. Holzworth, in his book *Historical Story Olmsted Township*, said of Bill Jenkins, "Few men equaled his dynamic energy."

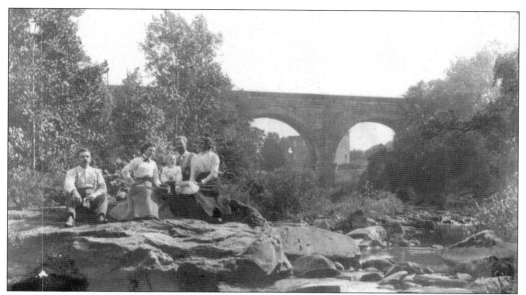

This photograph is of people enjoying East River Park with the railroad bridge over the Rocky River in the background. The river and the railroad played such an important part in the history and development of Olmsted Falls and are a major attraction of the park. A spur line once ran across what is now East River Park to the Barnum Quarry. Before the tracks were laid, stone was hauled by teams of horses and wagons to the railroad siding.

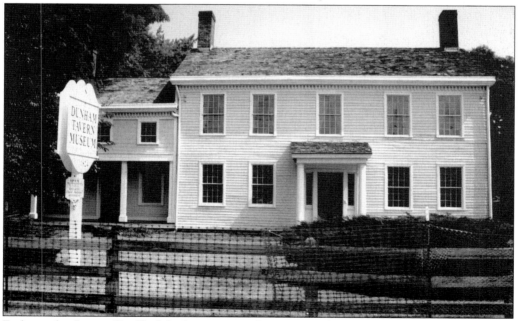

Early settler Lester Bradford had a stagecoach stop at a location of what would be today Nobottom and River Roads. There are no known photographs of the Bradford Stagecoach Inn. The photograph above is of Dunham Tavern Museum, built in 1824 and a west wing added in 1832. It is located at 6709 Euclid Avenue in Cleveland and does tell the story of life as it was for those early travelers.

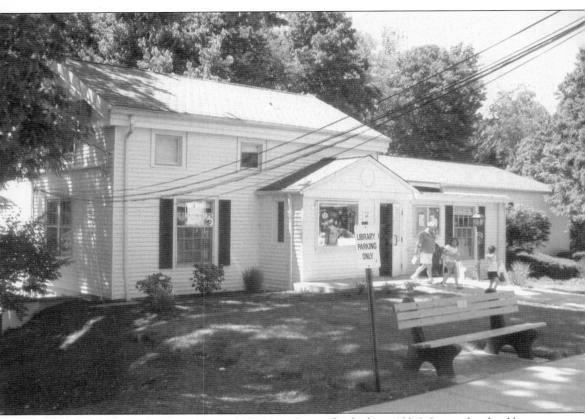

This is the Olmsted Falls Library at 7850 Main Street (built about 1834). It was the third location of the Newton P. Loomis House, an early settler of Olmsted Falls. John Loomis and his family came to what became Olmsted Falls in 1833 and built a log cabin on the banks of the Rocky River. It is believed that the Loomis family built the first finishing mill and factory on Plum Creek. It was located at 7865 Columbia Road where they also lived for a time. They then built a house at 8017 Columbia Road that was eventually moved to a location next to the Olmsted Community Church. It was in 1955 that the Olmsted Community Church donated the Loomis House to the community. It was then moved across the street to its present location to become the Olmsted Falls Library.

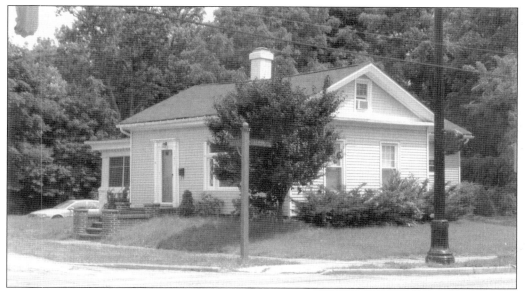

The building at 25477 Water Street is a New England one-and-a-half-story Greek Revival home. The Colonial Revival addition was added in the 1930s. The historic name is the John Lay home. Lay and his brother Joseph came to the Western Reserve in 1855 and became very successful and distinguished members of the community. It is believed that they built this home shortly after their arrival sometime in the late 1850s.

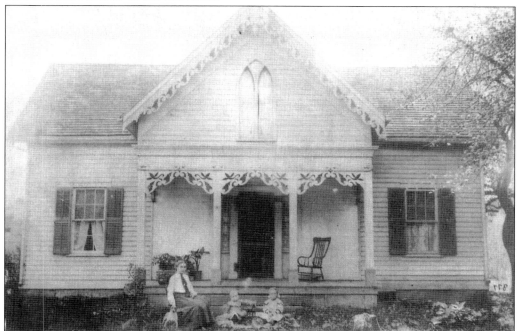

This photograph of 25419 Water Street was taken sometime after 1900. Originally built in the Gothic Revival style, today it displays three front-hipped dormers and a Greek Revival front entrance. The rock-faced sandstone foundation would suggest post–Civil War construction. In spite of the alterations over the years, the house retains much of its original character.

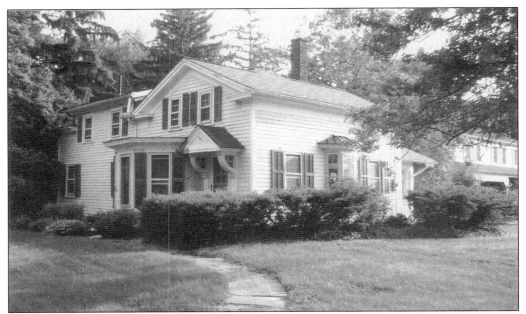

The Sanford and Clarissa Fitch Home was at 25347 Water Street (built about 1837). Sanford was one of the seven Fitch brothers who came to Olmsted with their parents in 1831 from East Windsor, Connecticut. It appears that the house originally faced Main Street. It has two facades, one facing Water Street, the other facing Main Street. Another feature of the house is an outside basement "tomahawk" door for protection against Native American attacks.

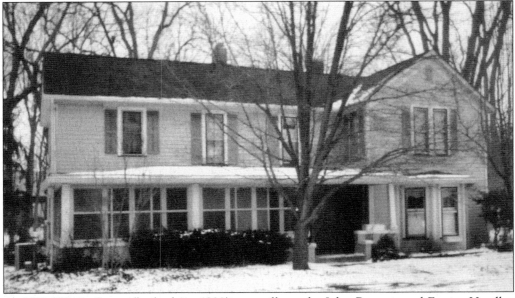

At 25334 Water Street (built about 1830) one will see the John Barnum and Eunice Hoadley House with the east wing added in the late 19th century, about 1880. One of the windows in the house has John Barnum's initials etched in it. As one reads through this book, the many accomplishments and contributions to the community of the Barnum and Hoadley families can be recognized.

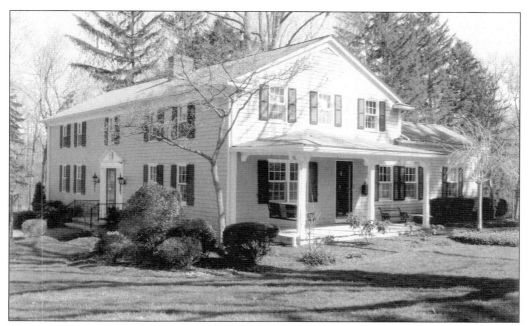

At 7707 Main Street at Water Street is the Major Lemuel Hoadley Home (built about 1836). Maj. Lemuel Hoadley, his wife, Chloe, and three children were one of the first parties of settlers from Waterbury, Connecticut, to come to the Western Reserve. Major Hoadley is credited with building a number of mills of the area. The home, built in the Greek Revival and neocolonial revival style, has been greatly enlarged over the years.

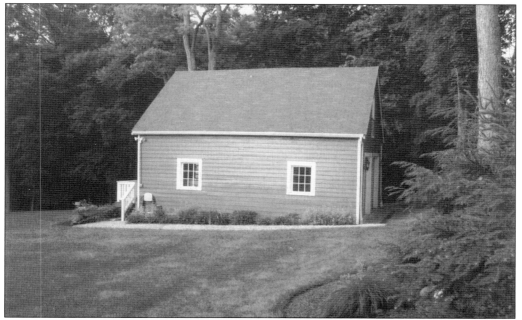

The Major Hoadley barn, just behind the house on Main Street, was the location of one of the many blacksmith shops in Olmsted before 1900. The blacksmith shop was operated by a man named Clarence Claysettle for many years.

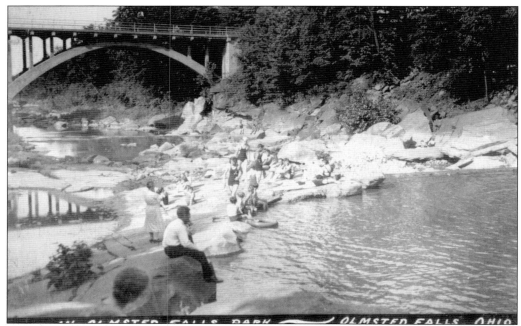

As one passes Fortier Park heading east on Water Street, the Rocky River will be crossed over. The photograph is from a postcard of swimmers in the Rocky River in what is today called Fortier Park. In the background is the second Water Street Bridge over the Rocky River.

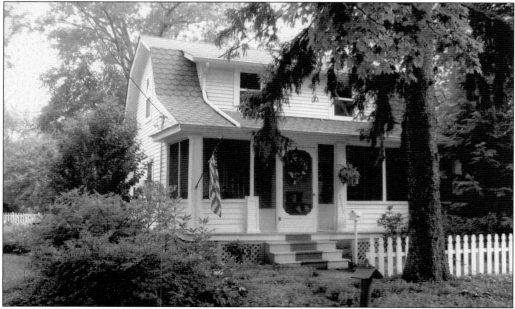

Another home located on the west side of Water Street at No. 25617 (built about 1920) is noted as a rare example of the Dutch Colonial Revival style of residential architecture in Olmsted Falls. The house dates from a period of intense growth as the community became more connected with Greater Cleveland through improved transportation connections. The house appears to be relatively unaltered over the years.

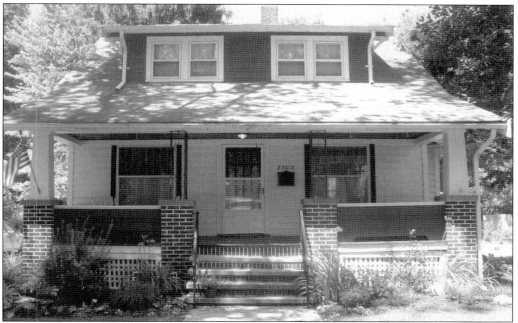

The structure at 25618 Water Street (built about 1920) was cited in the Ohio Historic Inventory as an especially fine example of bungalow architecture in Olmsted Falls. Typically a bungalow is a one-story house with gently pitched broad gables, a popular style from the 1890s to the 1940s. The large main gable roof swoops down in front to create a recessed front porch. A large, shed-roofed, front-facing gable creates space for second-floor bedrooms.

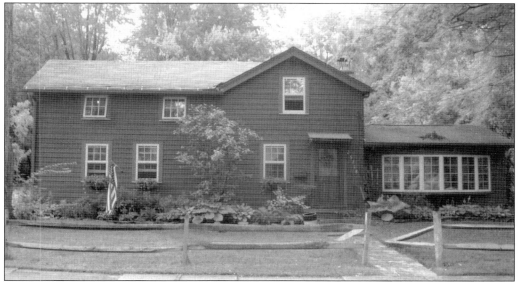

As one proceeds to the end of Water Street at Lewis Road, one will reach 25718 Water Street (built about 1850). The house is located in the Olmsted Falls Local Historic District. There have been a number of additions to the house, but they are basically compatible with its historic character. The one-story east wing is a newer addition. A recent, but attractive, two-car garage was built on the west side of the house.

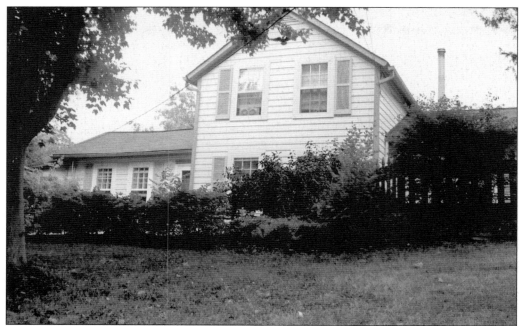

At 7659 River Road stands a house on a ridge overlooking the road. A home was built on the site before 1850. It appears much of the original home is intact. The *Atlas of Cuyahoga County, Ohio* shows the owners as A. O. Strong and James H. Strong. Dr. Pelton, who had an office on the second floor of the Peltz and Simmerer Hardware Store, also had an office in the home.

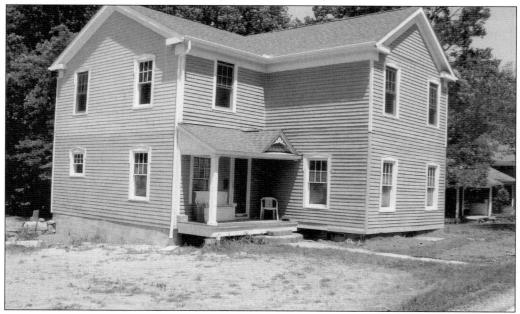

The home at 7650 River Road (built about 1855) belonged to Orvis C. Wright in 1855, according to Bernice Offenberg who lived in the house from 1919 through 1980. Her history of Olmsted Falls still serves as a good reference. In 1874, the house was owned by Alfred and Lillie Sabin. The property was recently purchased in 2000, and a second story was added to the building.

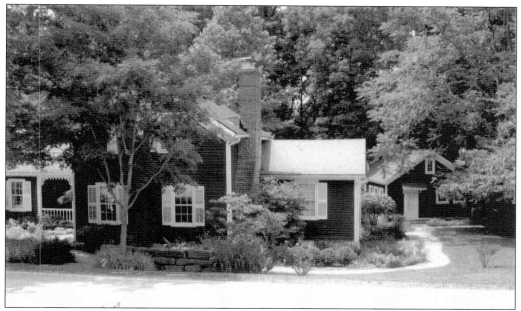

John Barnum Jr. sold land to David Wright, who built the house at 7634 River Road about 1869. It was built in the late Greek Revival style. The porch was later modified with Carpenter Gothic details. The small barn was removed and now serves as a library and guesthouse. In the rear yard, the 330-year-old red oak was named an Ohio champion in 2005.

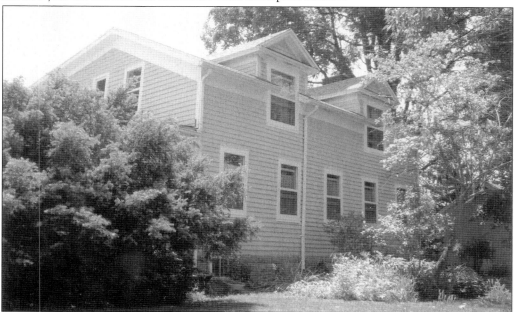

In 1831, Peter Kidney bought this land at 7623 River Road from Eliphalet Williams and sold it to H. K. Meiner, who built the house that same year. A subsequent owner, William Ponting, remodeled the house during his residence. The house is still a representative example of early pre–Civil War era housing of the area. The massive chimney and dormers were added in the mid-20th century.

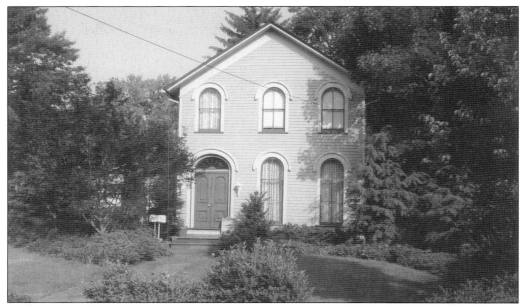

The Edward Kidney House was built at 7562 River Road about 1866 and is a good example of the Italianate style. His inventive genius produced many of the articles that developed his factory into one of the largest bending works of the Cleveland area. It was said that the story of his life could be called "A Man in Motion." He was a proprietor, boss, timber scout, purchasing agent, and sales manager.

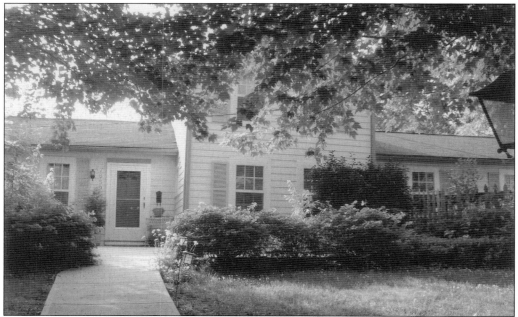

The John Neumann House was built about 1854 at 7569 River Road. The second owners were Calvin and Allie Romp. In 1900, it was the home of Dr. M. H. Westbrook. The parlor fireplace was constructed with river stone brought up from the west branch of the Rocky River, which runs below and behind the property.

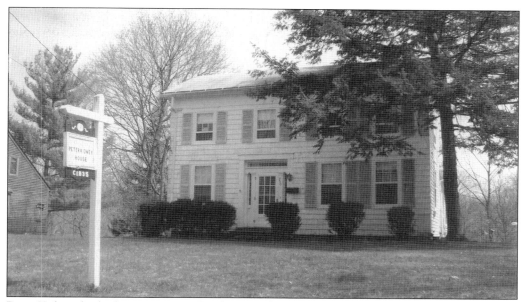

Peter Kidney built this impressive Greek Revival–style house at 7601 River Road to replace a one-room cabin that he built in 1833. The front part of the house was built in the late 1830s. In the spring of 1833 Peter Kidney and his wife, Asenath, and their baby, Thomas, came to Olmsted Falls by covered wagon. At the time there were no roads through the village, only the path along the river. He built a grist and iron mill along the river.

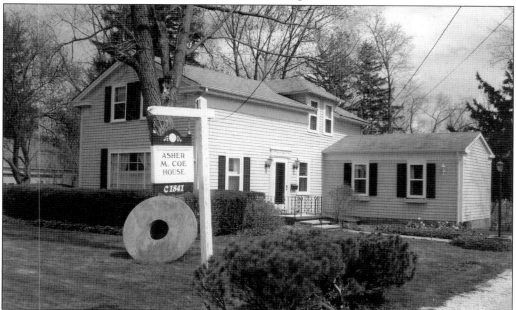

The Asher M. Coe House was built in the Greek Revival style, popular at the time, at 7557 River Road about 1840. Asher M. Coe was one of the early settlers who came to the Western Reserve in 1822. He was a real estate speculator, storekeeper, and government official. This house was built on the site of the Lay broom factory. The *Atlas of Cuyahoga County, Ohio* shows several small factories and a quarry along this section of the riverbank.

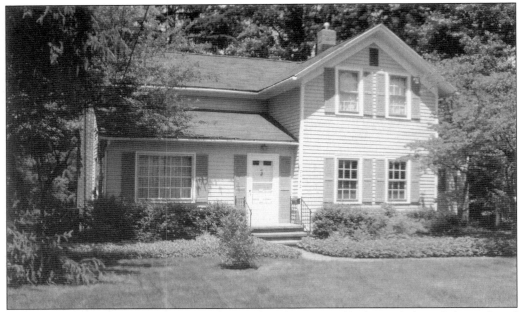

In 1874, the property at 7542 River Road was listed to F. Bradford. It is believed that referred to Freeman Bradford, who ran a dairy farm. In 1888, he moved to Cleveland to engage in the grocery business. Subsequent owners included Samuel Crittenden and his wife, Lemiral (Bradford); Charles Hyde and his wife, Daisy (Ruple) Hyde; Hubert Taylor; a Mr. Grover; John Bolton; and Mr. and Mrs. Charles Woodward, and it was owned for the last 40 years by Kenneth Alberta Gill.

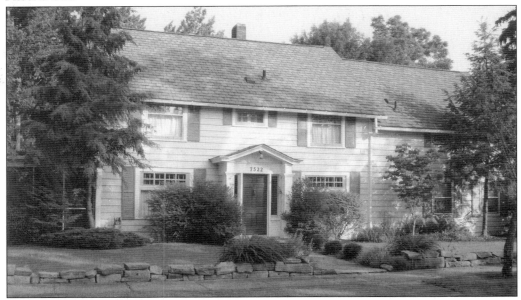

The C. B. Taylor House (built about 1850) was located 7522 River Road. According to the national register form, the original house was built around the 1842 frame schoolhouse that once stood on the village green. Other parts of the building appear to be built or added in the 1870s. It is one of the larger and better-preserved houses on River Road.

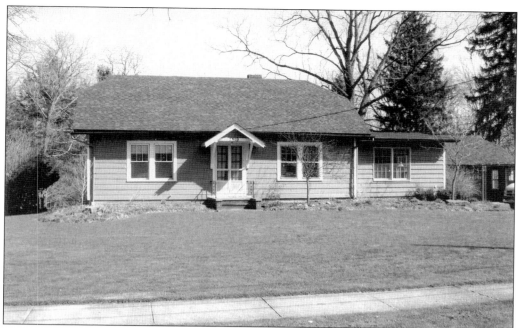

One of a number of bungalow-style, well-preserved homes of Olmsted Falls, 7519 River Road (built about 1920) relates to the early-20th-century development of Olmsted Falls. The building is included in the Olmsted Falls Local Historic District and Ohio Historic Inventory.

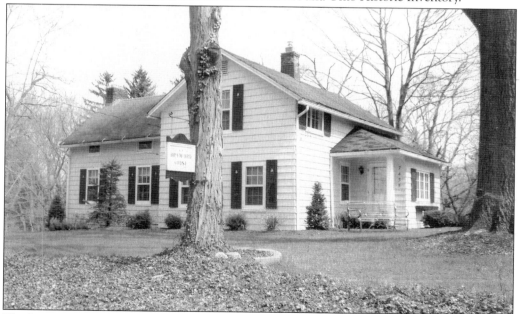

The house at 7435 River Road (built about 1851) was known as the Philo and Delight Bradford House. The building is cited as an example of vernacular pre–Civil War architecture in Olmsted Falls. It was owned by Ezra Bradford in the 1880s. The first Bradford to come to the Western Reserve was Hosea Bradford. He was a direct descendent of William Bradford, the second governor of Plymouth Colony in 1650.

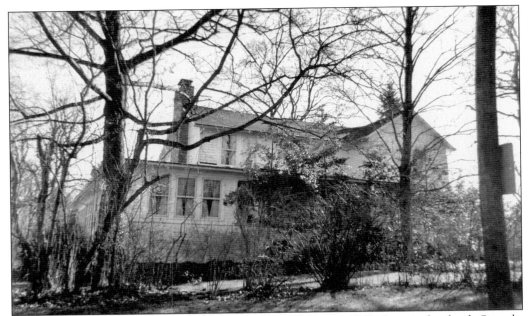

The David Owens home is located at 7473 River Road. Bernice Offenberg, in her book *Over the Years in Olmsted*, writes that from information from Helen K. Staten, the house was built by J. W. Williams in 1842. He sold the property in 1851 to Silas Jennings. There have been numerous owners of the property over the years.

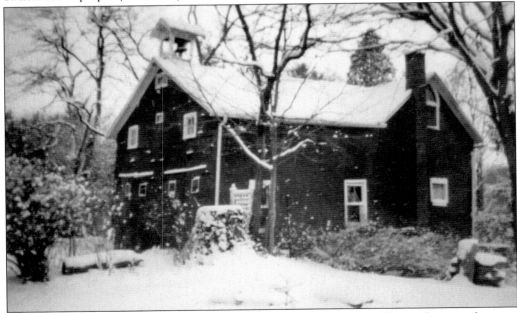

A number of historic barns on River Road remind us of the period of agriculture in the area. This barn (built about 1842) is located along the river behind 7473 River Road. County records show the construction of the home. Behind the barn is what is called a "Moses Cleaveland Tree," identified by the Early Settlers Association as a tree that stood when Moses Cleaveland founded the city.

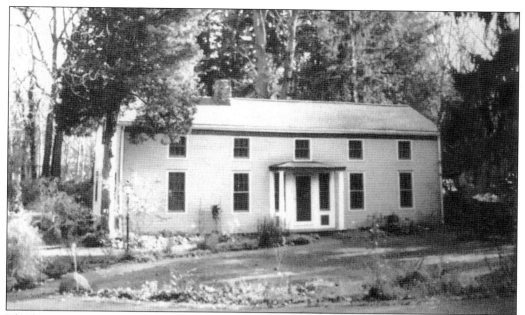

The home at 7407 River Road (built about 1842–1865) is known historically as the James and Lucy Strong House. The rear wing was once the first frame schoolhouse that stood on River Road in the 1840s. The owners of the property over the years sound like the business directory of Olmsted Falls, and even some American legends. Isaac and Margaret Fitch Rittenburg had "Wild" Bill Cody in their family tree. Cody Rittenburg was a second cousin of Wild Bill.

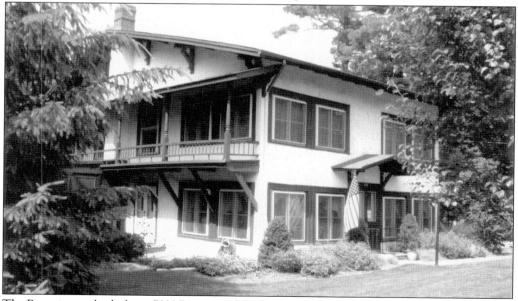

The Bavarian-style chalet at 7322 River Road (built about 1904) was constructed for Amber Heim, a Cleveland schoolteacher who envisioned a home for elderly women whose arts and crafts would support the home. When that dream failed, she started a sanitarium for boys with tuberculosis. She had a second, larger home built across the street, which became a tenement house, fell into disrepair, and was razed. Behind the home was the location of Bradford Stagecoach Inn.

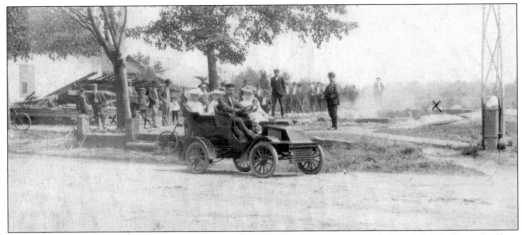

The parking lot of the Falls Veterinary Clinic was the location of the Odd Fellows hall at 8017 Columbia Road that was destroyed by fire in 1903. The photograph was taken on August 8, just after the fire. The hall was rebuilt, but because of the widening of the railroad tracks in 1909, the building was moved to 8154 Columbia Road. Charles Barnum built his home on the site in 1935. It is now the Falls Veterinary Clinic. Pictured in the car is Jake Flury, town marshal and blacksmith.

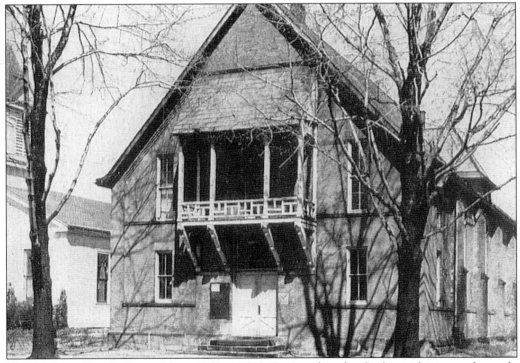

The former village hall stood from 1883 to 1939. Designed in the Gothic style, it was the pride of the town for many years. The 1940 neoclassical revival–style building at 7987 Columbia Road replaced it. The new town hall of 1940 was constructed with locally quarried Berea sandstone as part of a WPA project. In 2001, the Olmsted Falls administrative offices and police department moved to the 1916 Olmsted Falls school building at 26100 Bagley Road.

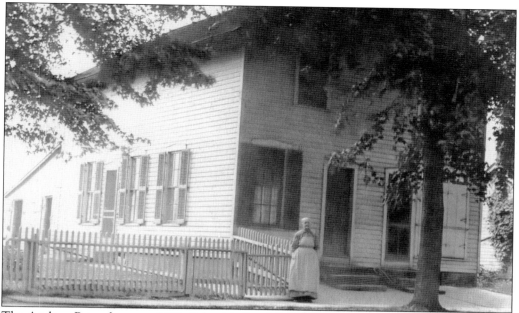

The Andrew Peters home at 8007 Columbia Road (built about 1878) is seen here as it appeared before it was turned to face south. Andrew Peters operated a cobbler shop and later a barbershop out of his home when it faced Columbia Road. It was not until 1946 that then owner Grover Imhoff moved the house to face south and removed the store window.

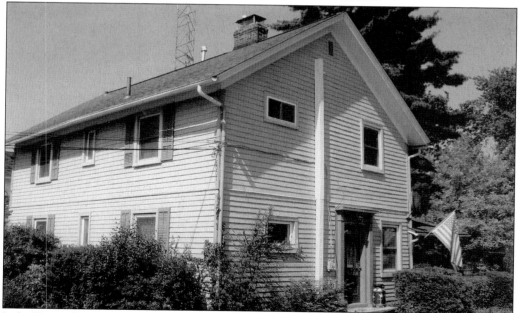

Imhoff served as superintendent of schools and as chairman of the town planning commission. He is credited with developing a realistic approach to zoning laws. His approach, as quoted in Walter F. Holzworth's book *Historical Story Olmsted Township*, was "that for zoning to be truly in the best interest of the entire community, it must be fluid and what applied to one generation or period, did not necessarily hold true to the next."

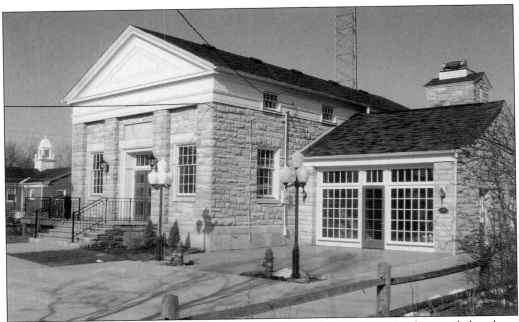

The new town hall at 7987 Columbia Road (built in 1940) by 1941 contained council chambers, a police station and jail, and the fire station. In 2001, the administrative offices and police department moved into the renovated 1916 Olmsted Falls school building at 26100 Bagley Road. The building, at the writing of this book, is being developed into a commercial building.

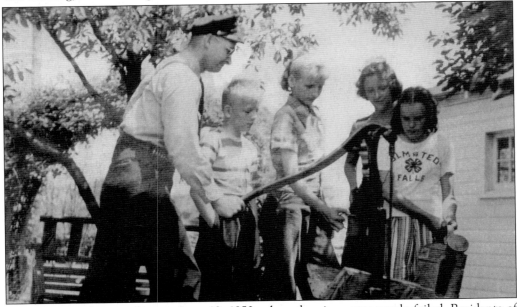

This photograph was taken on June 10, 1950, when the city water supply failed. Residents of Olmsted Falls had to rely on the old well. H. J. Nickels, assistant police chief, is shown pumping water for some needy residents. Seen here are, from left to right, Leonard Hawkins, age 10; Dorothy Smith, age 11; Nancy Pocsik, age 14; and Mary Ellen Chandler. (Cleveland State University, Cleveland Press Collection.)

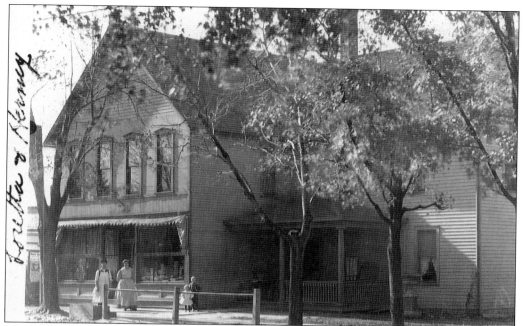

The Dodd-Fenderbosch Grocery Store building was located at 8820–8822 Columbia Road. In front of the store are Loretta and Henry Fenderbosch. This is a photograph of the original building on the site that dated from 1874, when Herman Fenderbosch opened a dry goods, millinery, and grocery store. The building was destroyed by fire in 1949, and a new building was built to continue as a grocery store. Today Parker Financial and Images Photography occupy the building.

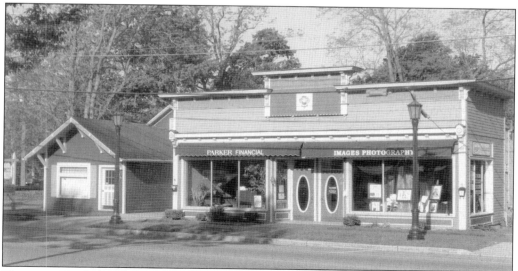

The name Fenderbosch has been associated with business and civic life of Olmsted Falls since 1872. In 1900, Fenderbosch sold his grocery interest to his son-in-law Arthur Dodd and opened a saloon that became the most popular in town. It perhaps became too popular, because in 1908, the village voted to close down all saloons in Olmsted Falls. Henry went back to the grocery business with his brother-in-law.

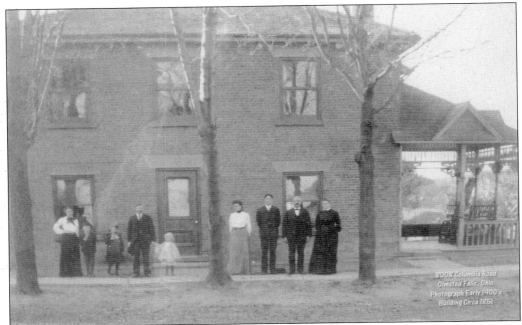

From evidence, it appears that the home at 8008 Columbia Road (built about 1853) was built by Thomas Broadwell. L. A. Harmon owned the property for only a short period of time. In addition, on the south side of the house below a window, a brick bears the initials T. B. The bricks used to build this home were from the Bradford Brick Factory owned by Lester and Eastman Bradford. The brick factory was located near the Chestnut Grove Cemetery on Lewis Road. Their father, Hosea Bradford, came to the area in 1820. Herman Fenderbosch was the ninth owner of the property. Fenderbosch had his saloon and pool hall next door. After the community was voted dry, he opened a dry goods, millinery, and grocery store in the former saloon and pool hall.

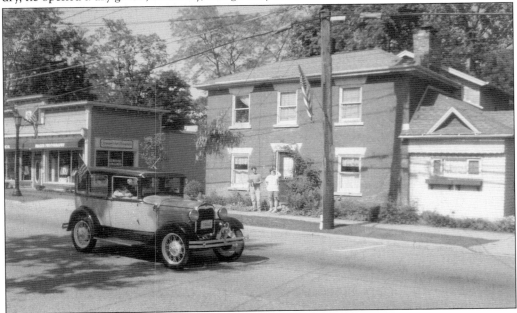

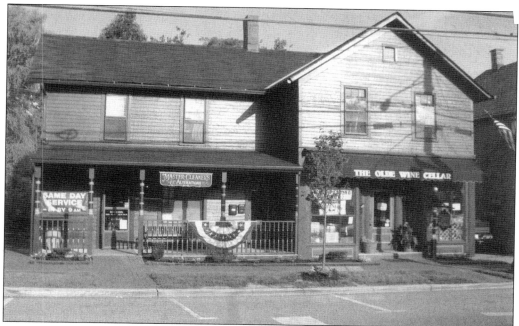

The George Dryden General Store located at 7990–7994 Columbia Road (built about 1860) had many uses over the years, but it is most remembered as a saloon and pool hall. Herman Fenderbosch opened the saloon and pool hall next door to his home. He retired, and his son Henry took over the saloon. In 1908, the village voted to close all saloons. Henry then joined his brother-in-law, Arthur Dodd, and opened a grocery store at 8820–8822 Columbia Road.

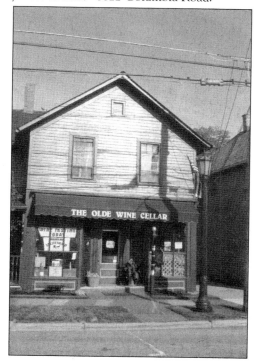

In 1945, Andrew Froehlich bought this building and opened a shoe repair shop in the saloon and a dry cleaning store that was managed by his son Walter in what was the pool hall. Today the dry cleaning tradition continues as Master Cleaners and Alterations. To the north side of the building is the Olde Wine Cellar.

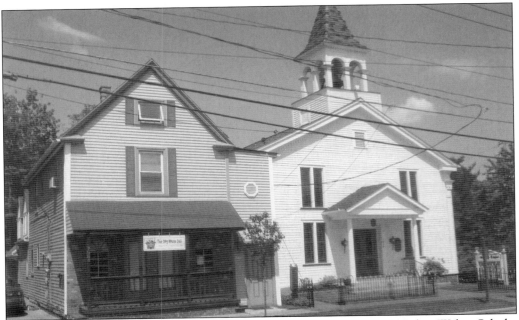

Schultz's barbershop and home was at 7984 Columbia Road. It was in 1928 that Walter Schultz came to Olmsted Falls. His first barbershop was at 8028 Columbia Road just north of the railroad tracks. He stayed in business at the site for 39 years. Today it is the Dog House Deli, Ohio's newest bakery and deli catering to mankind's four-legged friends that sells natural and organic dog food.

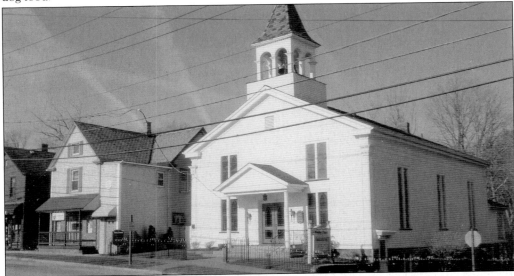

Seen here is 7970 Columbia Road (built about 1852). It was in 1843 that a Methodist society was organized in Olmsted Falls. By 1852, the church was built. In 1917, the Methodist and the Congregational churches merged, using the Methodist church for services and the Congregational church for community activity. In 1956, the Olmsted Falls Masonic Lodge purchased the church as a meeting hall. Clint Williams bought the building in 2001 and undertook its restoration.

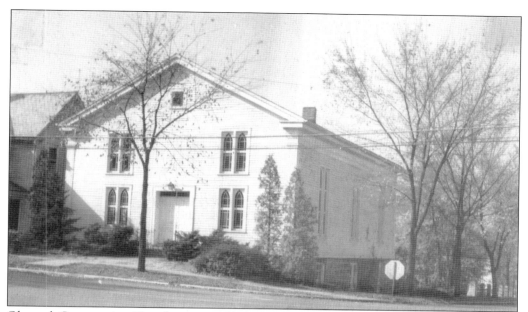

Olmsted Community Church was established in 1917, but it can trace its history to the First Congregational Church of Olmsted that was established in 1835. They joined with the Methodist church that had organized in 1843. They now form the Federation of Methodist and Congregational Churches of Olmsted Falls, Ohio. As a result of the merger in Olmsted Falls of the Congregational church and the Methodist church, they are now called Olmsted Community Church and are affiliated with the United Church of Christ. It was on May 24, 1923, that they officially became chartered as the Olmsted Community Church. The photograph below is of the groundbreaking for the education center. Looking west, the old church that is now the nondenominational wedding chapel can be seen. (Olmsted Community Church collection.)

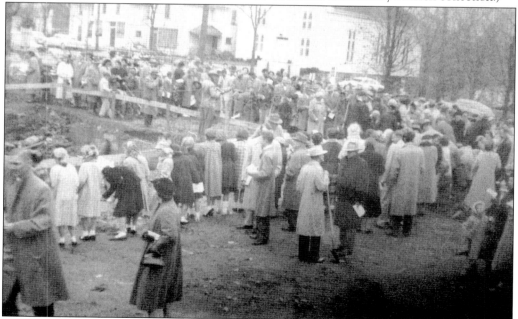

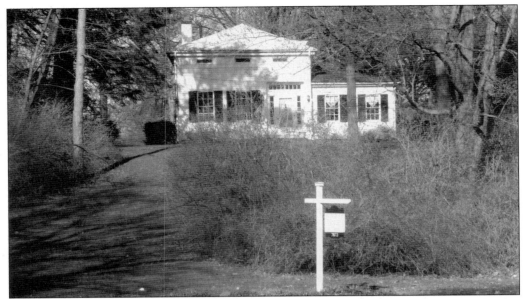

The Dr. Charles and Julia Carter Northrop Home (built about 1842) is located at 7872 Columbia Road. Alonzo Carter, son of Lorenzo Carter, the first permanent settler of Cleveland, built the house for his daughter Julia Carter Northrop in the Greek Revival style on a hill with an imposing front entrance. At one time, the estate included over 100 acres. The home has been added to the National Register of Historic Places for its history and architecture.

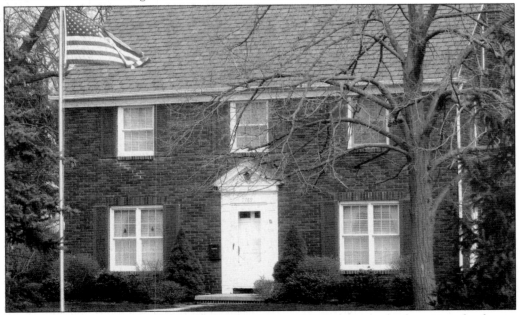

The Harding home (built about 1936), 7769 Columbia Road, is on the location of a former boot-making and shoemaking shop and home of Cornelius DeRooi, who came to the village of Olmsted Fall with his wife and son, Andrew, in 1864. In 1890, Andrew succeeded his father and added a grocery and general store to the shoe shop. Andrew's daughter Clara married Harry Harding, son of Charles Harding. Their children were Amelia, Charles, and Clara.

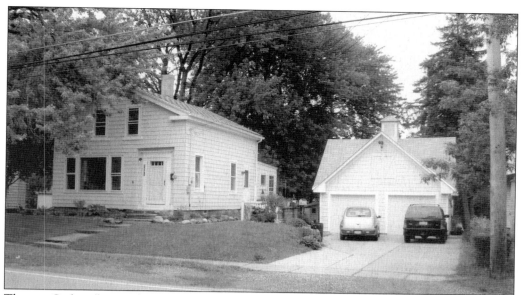

Thomas Stokes (known by members of the community as the lumberman) owned the house at 7835 Columbia Road, and it is believed that he built a connection from his sawmill and lumberyard to the home. It became known as the Alcott and Stokes lumberyard and builder supply, the first of Olmsted Falls. The waterfalls that supplied the power for the mill are the falls for which Olmsted Falls is named.

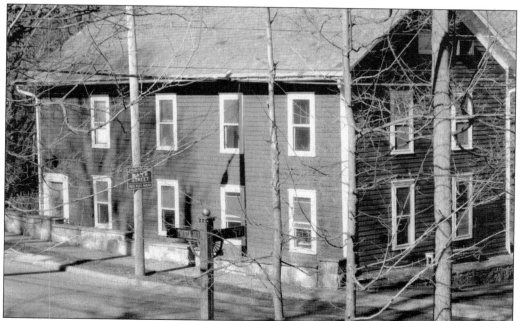

The house at 7835 Columbia Road is known as the Grand Army of the Republic (GAR) home (built about 1875). It was in 1887 that the GAR organized and used the upper story of the building. Stokes was selected as post commander. Sylvester Alcott and Stokes used the lower floor or basement to store lumber. For a time, Peter Kidney used the second floor for a chair factory after he retired from his tool-making business on River Road.

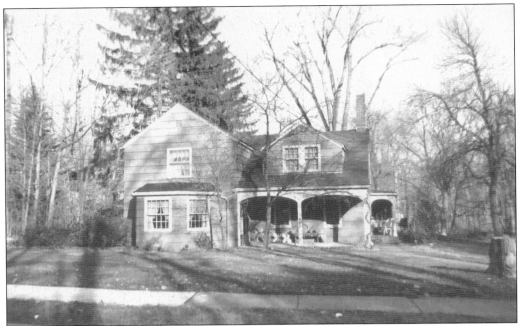

The Joseph Olmsted Loomis home (built about 1843) was located at 7865 Columbia Road. It was in 1832 that Joseph Sr. and his oldest sons, John and Joseph, came to Olmsted from Connecticut. In 1843, Joseph Sr. and Newton Loomis purchased land from Edward Hamlin that included Plum Creek Falls and built what they called a planing or finishing mill. The mill was near or on the site of the Alcott and Stokes Mill.

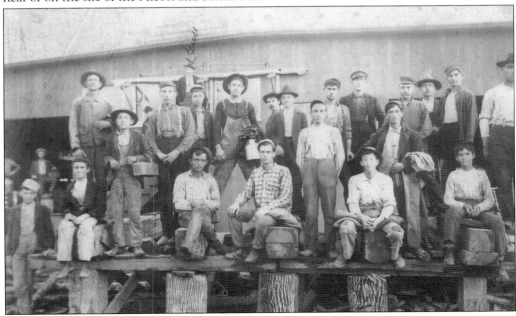

The quarries and mills provided work for many of the men of Olmsted Falls. Quarries, when in full operation, employed from 50 to 85 men. The Columbia Quarry that opened in 1820 employed 85 men at its peak. As can be seen from the photograph, they were both men and boys.

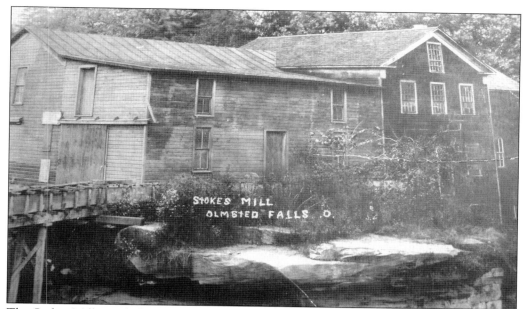

The Stokes Mill stood along Plum Creek behind 7835 Columbia Road. It was later known as the Alcott and Stokes Mill. The remains of the mill can be seen at the end of the Dan Waugh Trail behind the Olmsted Falls Library. In 1920, the mill house was torn down. The first mill near or on this location was the Loomis Mill built by Joseph Sr. and his son in 1844. (Bill Nickels collection.)

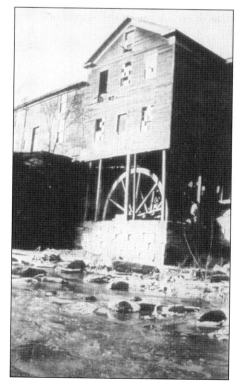

This is a photograph of the 1844 Loomis Mill that stood on or near the site of the Stokes Mill. Joseph Sr. and his son Newton P. built a planing mill to aid in the production of chairs, tables, and coffins. In 1864, the Loomis family sold the mill site to Levi and Sylvester Alcott. (Bill Nickels collection.)

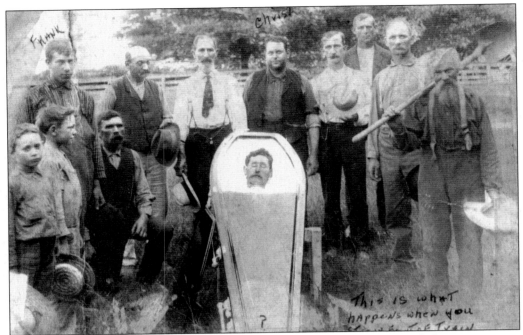

Working in the quarries and mills was arduous and dangerous work, and there were some casualties. The man in the coffin was hit by a train when at work; all of his fellow workers have at least removed their hats. This photograph was taken sometime in the 1870s. (Bill Nickels collection.)

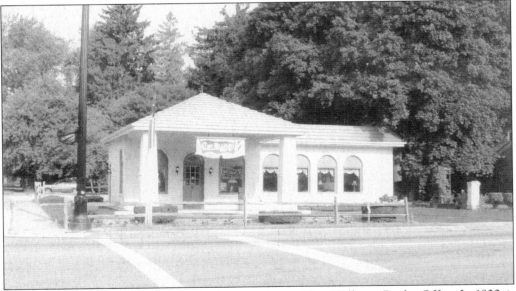

The building at 7684 Columbia Road operates today as Clint Williams Realty Office. In 1830, it was the location of the Chauncey Mead harness shop, an important location during the horse and buggy days. It became a dress shop. In 1927, in the automobile age, Leonard Parker opened a Shell gasoline and service station and continued that operation until the late 1960s. In 1972, the property was purchased by Clint Williams.

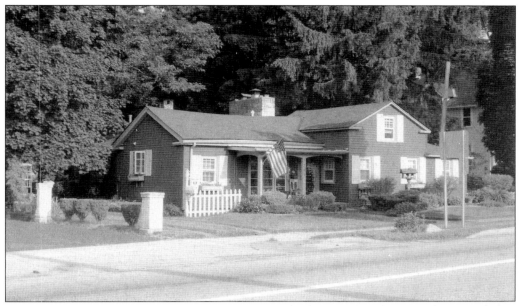

The Chauncey Mead home is located at 7674 Columbia Road (built about 1830). He settled in Olmsted Township in the early 1830s. He started a shoemaker business at this address. Then with his son he built a harness factory and store at 7684 Columbia Road. He was elected mayor of Olmsted Falls in 1858. The first meeting of the Congregation church was held in this house on April 16, 1835.

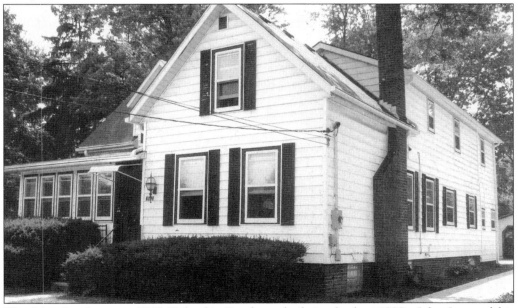

The John Lay home at 7642 Columbia Road was built in the late 1800s. John Lay and his brothers, Samuel and Joseph, came to the Western Reserve in 1855. John and his brothers started a farm implements business and ran a bending works and a cheese box factory on River Road along the Rocky River. John served as mayor of Olmsted Falls in the 1860s and 1890s. The building is listed on the National Register of Historic Places.

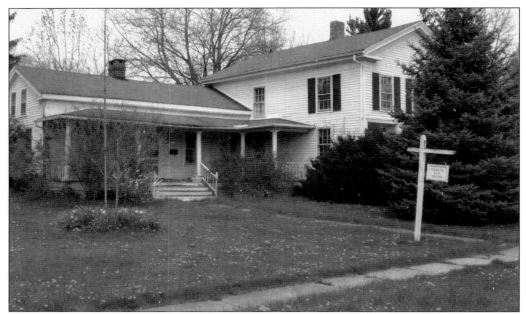

The Samuel Lay Jr. home was built about 1845 in the Greek Revival style at 7622 Columbia Road. Both Samuel Sr. and Samuel Jr. lived in the house. The business competition between the Lay brothers and Edward Kidney helped ignite creative competition that benefited the community.

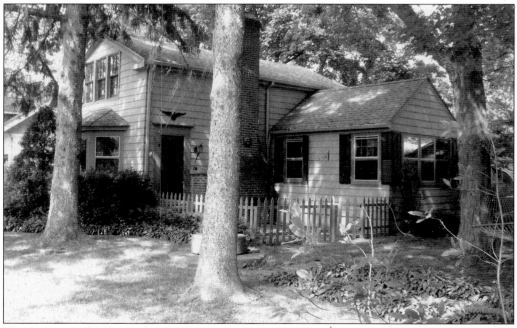

The home of Thomas Stokes, a prominent Olmsted Falls resident and Civil War veteran who pioneered the development of early threshing equipment, is located at 7609 Columbia Road. He also owned the home at 7835 Columbia Road along the sawmill. The house at 7609 Columbia Road was later the home of Ray Hecker, who operated the first gas station in town at the beginning of the automobile age.

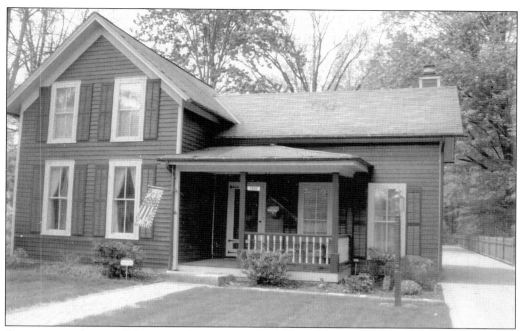

County records record the time of construction of 7582 Columbia Road as 1890. The building was in a state of disrepair when purchased by Mike Potts, who in the early 1990s undertook its restoration. Research by Margaret and Bob Potts show that the house appears to have been built by a Barney Hyman, who owned the property from 1885 to 1889.

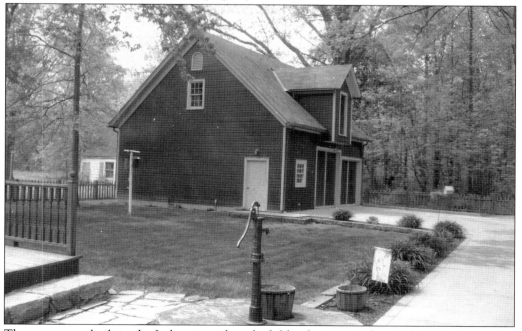

The garage was built in the Italianate style to look like the carriage house that may have stood on the property many years ago. The second floor of the garage served as an office for Potts Construction, which built the barn in the 1990s.

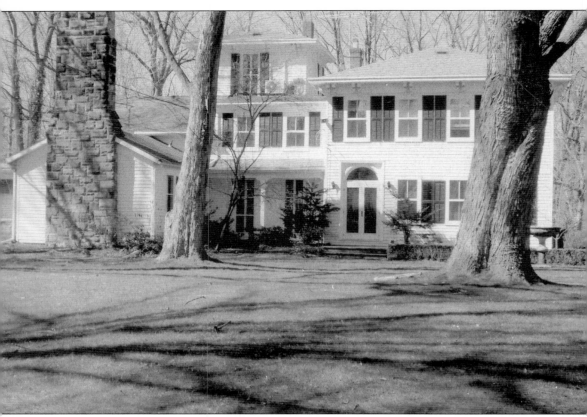

It was in the fall of 1810 that John Adams Sr., with his family, left Connecticut to seek a home in the wilds of the Western Reserve. The story of the treacherous journey is recounted in Bernice Offenberg's book *Over the Years in Olmsted*. In 1820, they built a cottage at 7315 Columbia Road at Nobottom Road. It is believed that the cottage that makes up the center of the house establishes it as the oldest home in the community. The original building was a 25-by-32-foot cottage. The center tower was built by Arthur Gray, who owned the building in the 1860s. His daughter Frances Gray was born in the tower room in 1866. Adams was born in Waterbury and carried the name of the first vice president and second president of the United States. Adams served as president from 1797 to 1801. In 1935, Theodore TeGrotenhuis, of the prominent Olmsted Falls family, purchased the property. It seems appropriate they purchased the house, since the name TeGrotenhuis means "the big house" in Dutch.

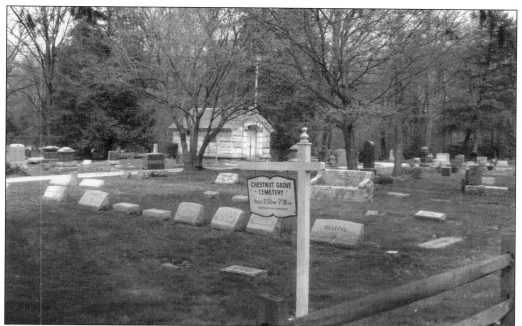

The Chestnut Grove Cemetery is located on Chestnut and Lewis Roads, overlooking the Rocky River. In 1854, the township trustees decided that the township needed another burial plot near the village. In 1887, the mausoleum was built of rock-faced sandstone, an impressive centerpiece for a cemetery. Like many old cemeteries there are ghost stories, and Chestnut Grove is not an exception. The Upper Midwest Ghost Society provides the details about a woman accused of witchcraft who was executed and buried in the cemetery in an unmarked grave. It has been said that strange things happen next to the tree where she was buried. The new Chestnut Grove Cemetery is located on Lewis Road. It is a much larger plot of land and located across from East River Park.

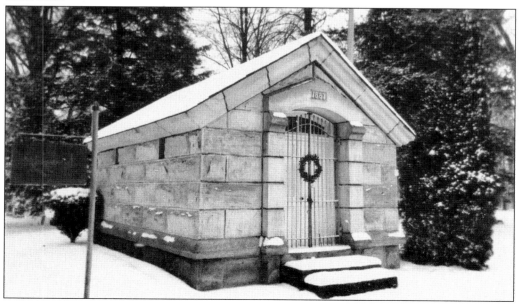

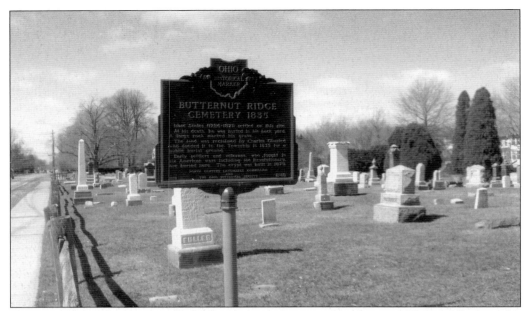

Butternut Ridge Cemetery is the oldest cemetery in township 6, range 15. Isaac Scales, who settled on the site, died in 1821. He was the first to be buried in what became the cemetery. In 1835, Charles Olmstead, who had reclaimed the land, conveyed the land to the village trustees to be used as a burial ground. Inscribed on the headstones is the history of those early settlers.

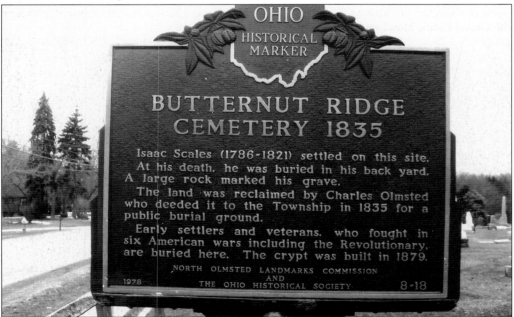

The Ohio historic marker at the cemetery in part reads, "Early settlers and veterans, who fought in six American wars including the Revolutionary, are buried here." There are a total of 80 Civil War veterans interred in Butternut Ridge and Coe Ridge Cemeteries in North Olmsted. In Olmsted Falls, there are 11 veterans in Chestnut Grove and St. Mary's Cemeteries. The sandstone crypt was built in 1879.

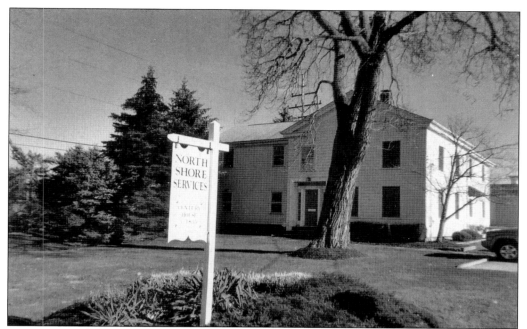

The Dryden Knowlton home was built about 1835 at 7993 Lewis Road. In 1834, Capt. C. P. Dryden and his wife, Harriet, purchased land on what is now Lewis Road where they built their home. Their daughter, Hanna, married Dr. A. P. Knowlton, whose father was probably the first resident physician of Olmsted Township. It is believed that the seminary building that is now the Grand Pacific Hotel was on the Dryden property.

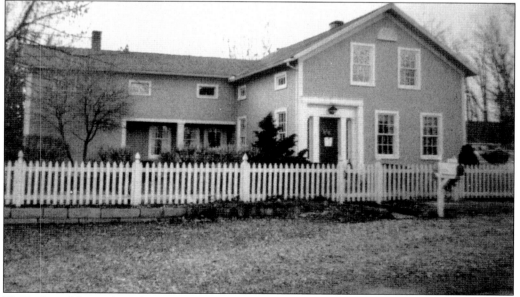

Eli Fitch and his wife, Sabra, came from East Windsor, Connecticut, to Olmsted Township in 1831. They built a log cabin then replaced it with this home at 8566 Lewis Road (about 1834). It was built as a farmhouse in the Greek Revival style popular at the time. The Fitch property appears in the *Atlas of Cuyahoga County, Ohio* as 68 acres.

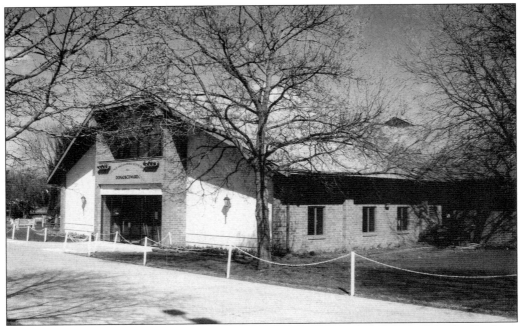

Driving south on Columbia Road just before entering Olmsted Falls, the Danube Swabian German American Cultural Center, organized in 1958, can be seen to the right. It grew from a small building on West 140th Street near Lorain Road that is now a VFW hall. Today there are 20 beautiful acres with a large hall that can seat over 600 people in the grand ballroom.

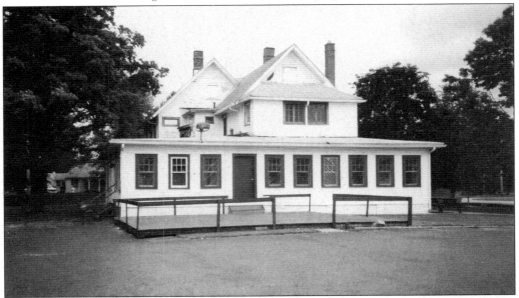

Lenau Park, as it is called, is the home of various groups organized around common interests that include folk dancers, singers, musicians, bowlers, tennis players, soccer players, skiers, golfers, handcrafters, chess players, and a seniors group. The name Lenau comes from Nikolaus Lenau (1802–1850), a German poet who came to America and settled near Bucyrus. The photograph is of the Ritter home that once stood on the property.

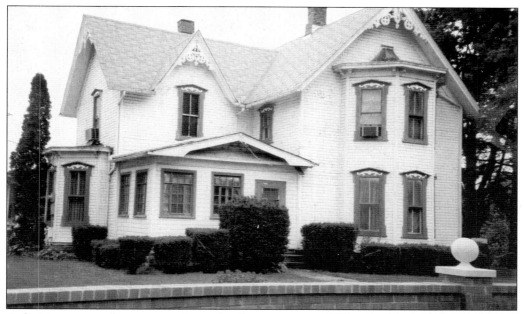

A decision was made at a general membership meeting in 1979 to build a hall. Joseph Holzer, former president of Danube Swabians and current director of operations, was one of those responsible for the construction of the center. The building was dedicated on May 17 and 18 in 1986. The photograph is of the dining hall of the Ritter Restaurant and catering business that was on the south side of the building.

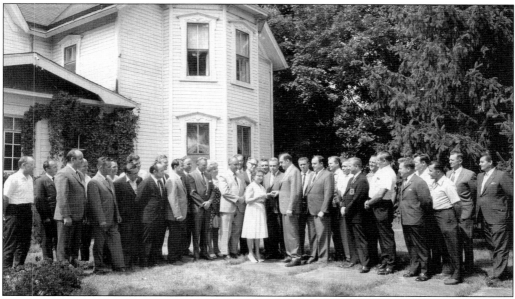

The house that stood on the property was called Ritter's Farm Dinner House. Elsie Ritter ran a restaurant and catering business. The first owners of the property were Joseph Gibson and his wife, Margaret. Gibson built the second dam for the Ed Damp Grist Mill in 1883. Officers, members, and friends gather with Ritter to turn over the title to the property to the German American Cultural Center.

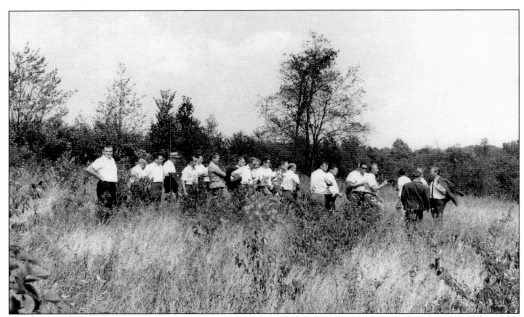

The Danube Swabians are people who colonized land along the Danube River at the end of the Ottoman Wars. That colonization began in 1722. Unlike many American pioneers who often traveled westward in wagons, those pioneers journeyed on the Danube River by barge. Members and friends with the vision and memory of history look over the land of the overgrown farm. Today one can see a soccer field and beautiful grounds.

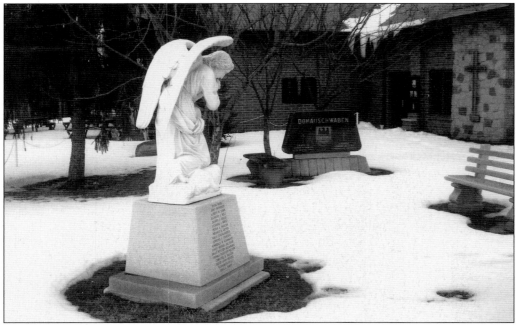

The shrine outside the main hall is to remind people of the suffering of the people called Danube Swabians who, as a result of World War II and the advancement of Communism, were persecuted through no fault of their own, just because of their German origin.

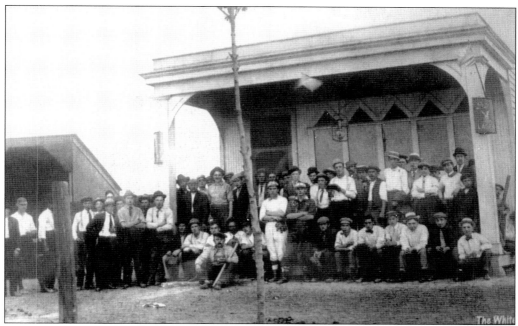

The photograph above is of the White Elephant Saloon taken sometime in early 1900. It was located on Columbia Road between Olmsted and Westview. Working at the quarries, the farms, and the railroad was hard work, and the saloons provided an outlet. It looks as if it may have been free beer night at the White Elephant Saloon. Below is a photograph of the Blue Hen also taken about the same time as the White Elephant Saloon. It was also located on Columbia Road south of Bagley Road. The men in front of the saloon may be wondering where all the customers are; maybe they should check the White Elephant Saloon. In May 1888, the township voted to establish local option laws that could close down saloons. In 1890, there were three saloons within the village limits; by 1908, there were none and the village voted dry. (Bill Nickels collection.)

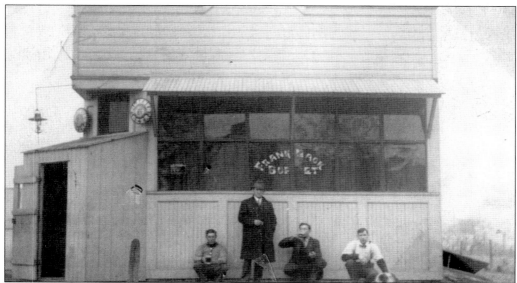

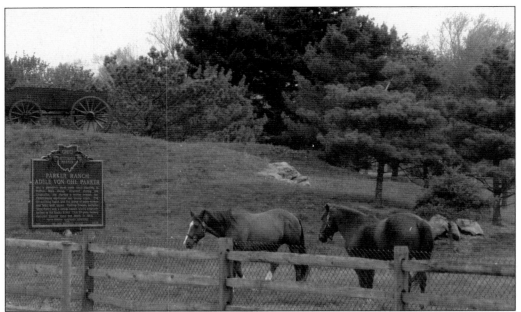

In 1928, Mr. Parker and his wife, Adele, and her sister, Winnanah von Ohl, came to Cleveland as performers in a horse act in vaudeville shows. It was one the largest horse acts on the vaudeville stage until the Great Depression caused it to close. In 1929, they bought the Giesel farm on Mastick Road and established a ranch that became widely known for its annual horse and Wild West shows.

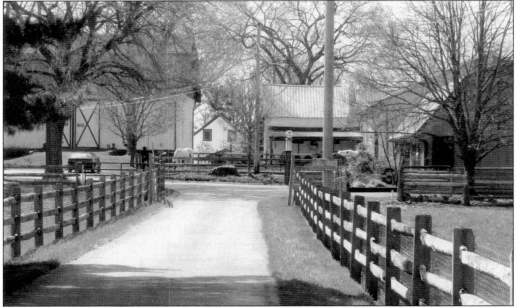

At an early age, the von Ohl sisters starred in Buffalo Bill's Wild West shows, as well as in motion pictures and vaudeville. Winnanah rode a horse as it dove into a tank of water. Adele's act on a Lipizzaner horse was a great hit. She was quite a lady and one of the most colorful personalities of the Olmsted area.

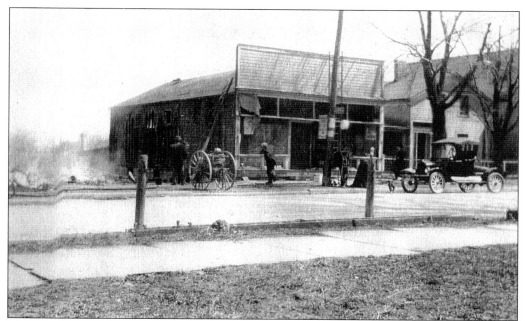

The fire that occurred on the east side of the Columbia Road business district in 1913 was one of the most disastrous fires in the village. It was not until January 1926 that a Model T truck with a water pump was purchased. In 1929, the department received a Seagrave pumper fire engine. After the fire, the Barnum Grocery Store was built on the site. (Bill Nickels collection.)

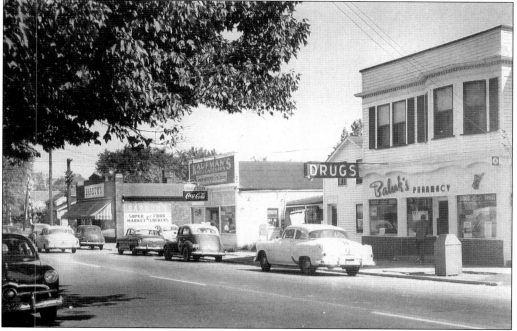

Here is a view looking northeast at the business district of Olmsted Falls in the late 1940s or early 1950s. All of the buildings in the photograph are now gone. Only the foundation of the Barnum Grocery Store remains today.

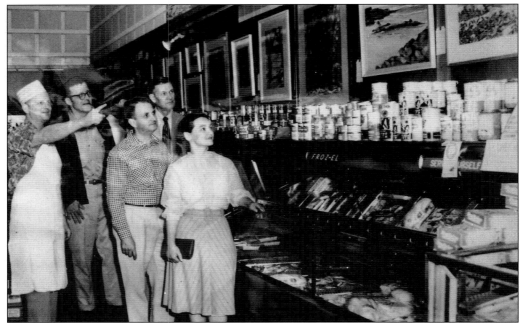

Charles Barnum was proud of his store. This photograph from the Cleveland State University Cleveland Press Collection was taken on June 13, 1953. Seen here are, from left to right, grocer Charles Barnum, Audrey Billings, Herbert Erisman, Lloyd Westbrook, and Mrs. Jo Natko.

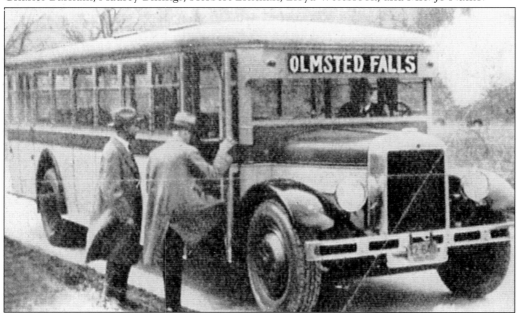

In 1927, the Cleveland Olmsted Falls Bus Line began operation, consisting of a schedule of half-hour service during rush hour and one-hour service during the midday. By 1928, six buses were in operation from the village to Cleveland. Passenger train service from Olmsted Falls to Cleveland was limited to five trips a day on what was called the "Plug." That service ended in 1949. (Cleveland State University, Cleveland Press Collection.)

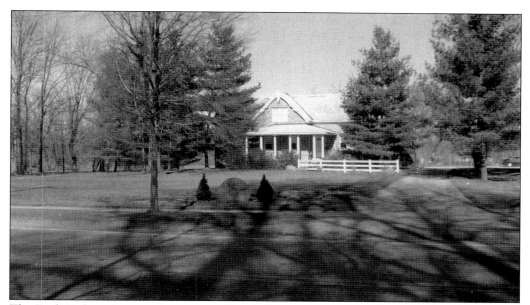

The Fitch-Perkins farm (built about 1860) at 7555 Columbia Road is a rare example of Gothic Revival–style architecture in Olmsted Falls. The building has been altered over the years for the changing times but has been well-preserved, and for many years it was an important farm of the village. Fitch and Perkins were major players in the development of the area.

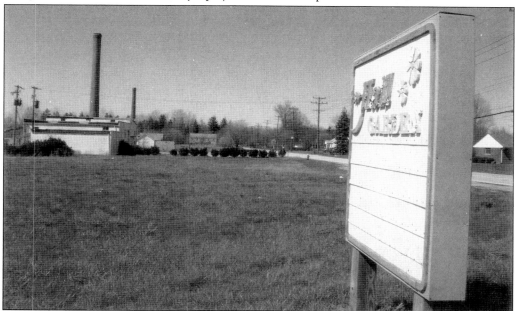

There is little left of Hall Garden greenhouse today except for the sign and some remaining deteriorating greenhouse structures. Ohio's greenhouse roots can be traced to European immigrants who settled in the area during the late 1800s and early 1900s and developed greenhouses to lengthen Ohio's growing season. The Hall name is still very prominent in the area. Next to the former greenhouses is Hall's Quality Meat Market located between McKenzie and Stearns Roads.

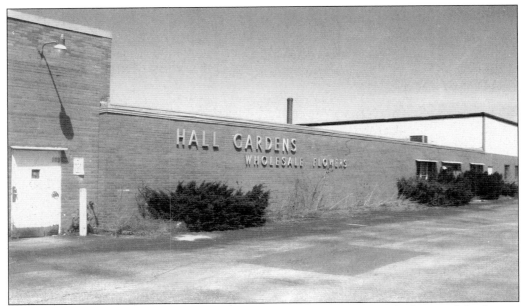

George Hall, who was known in the town as "Greenhouse George," had one of the largest areas under glass in the township. It was located on Cook and McKenzie Roads. By the 1940s, Olmsted Falls and Olmsted Township and the Schaaf Road area of Cleveland were the two areas with the greatest concentration of greenhouses in the United States. All that remains today of the Hall greenhouse is the sign and deteriorating structures.

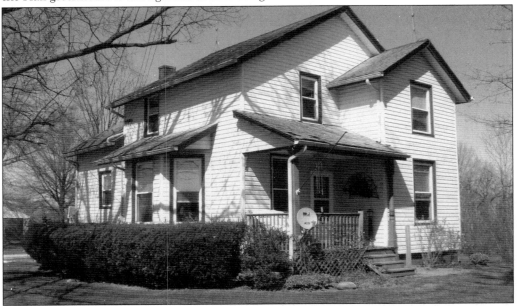

The Hall homestead and barn (built about 1883) still stand today at the corner of McKenzie and Stearns Roads. The first of the Hall family to come to Olmsted Township was George, who came to the sparsely settled area in the mid-1800s. The greenhouse business still is alive in Olmsted Falls and the surrounding area with Uncle John's Plant Farm, Hansen's Greenhouse, Schuster's Greenhouse, Exotica Greenhouse, and others that are worth the visit.

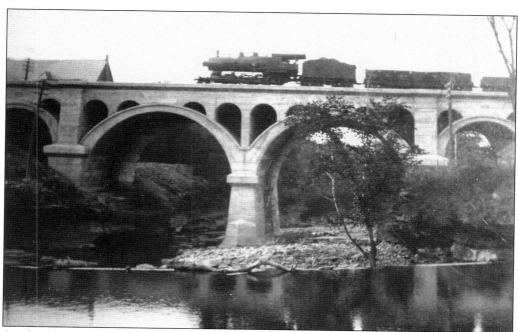

At the height of the construction of the railroad, over 4,000 men labored on work crews stretching from Cleveland to Columbus clearing trees, grading roadbeds, and building bridges and stone retaining walls. The work was almost entirely done by Irish, German, and Polish immigrant labor. That was evident in Olmsted Falls since Bagley Road was once called Irish Road; the other end was Dutch Road. The photograph above is of the Cleveland, Cincinnati, Chicago and St. Louis Railroad formed in 1889. (Above, Bill Nickels collection.)

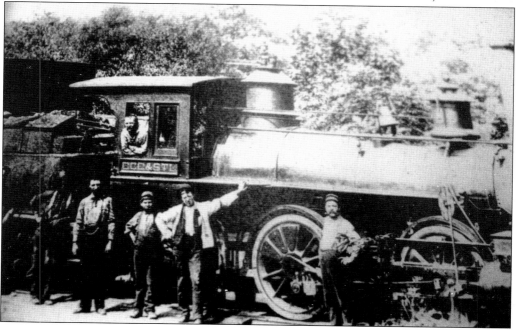

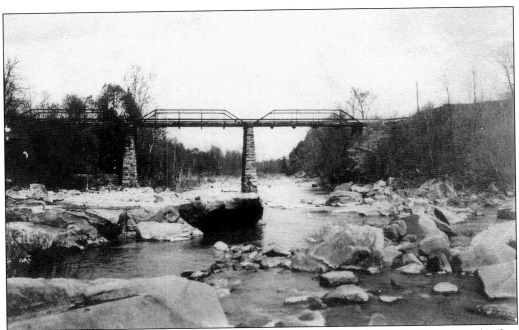

This photograph postcard of the Rocky River Bridge was taken on March 25, 1913. The first Bagley Road Bridge over the Rocky River was completed in 1870. The road became known as Irish Road because a man named William Murphy owned the land where the road began in Berea, and James Hickey owned the land in Olmsted Falls where the road ran through.

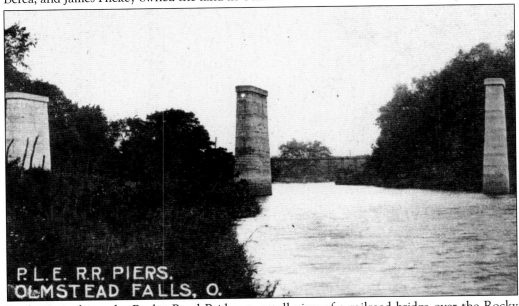

Looking south on the Bagley Road Bridge, two tall piers of a railroad bridge over the Rocky River can be seen. It was the Pittsburgh and Lake Erie Railroad that bought the right-of-way. The land was graded for tracks between Lorain and Berea in 1903 and 1904. Work was halted when they ran into unexpected swampy terrain near Berea, and the line was abandoned in 1905 without the track ever being laid.

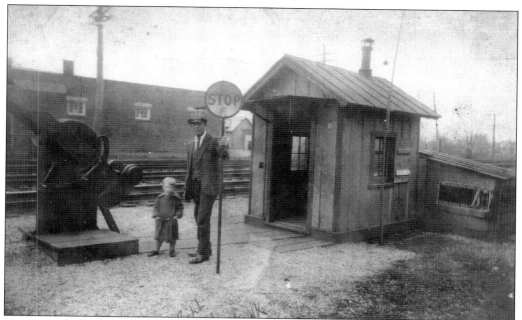

The Columbia Road crossing is seen here in 1940. As early as 1904, the village council, because of casualties at the crossing, insisted that a flagman be on duty at all times to warn of approaching trains. This photograph is of young Bill Nickels getting special attention from his uncle Frank, who was the crossing guard. (Bill Nickels collection)

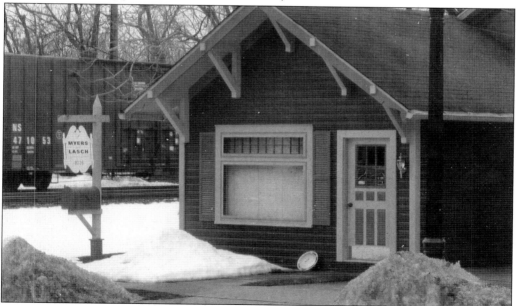

The location of the first railroad depot and flag station was at 8026 Columbia Road. The new station was built on Division Street and was later moved to 25802 Garfield Road. It stands today as an important landmark of Olmsted Falls. In 1928, Walter Schultz opened a barbershop at 8026 Columbia Road; he later moved his barbershop and residence to 7984 Columbia Road. Today 8026 Columbia Road is the office of Myers and Loach Incorporated.

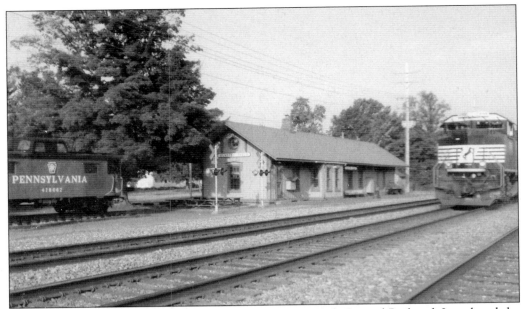

The Olmsted Falls train depot was built in 1877 by New York Central Railroad. It replaced the small flag station that was located on Columbia Road. Passenger service ended in 1949 and freight service in 1952. The depot was purchased by the Cuyahoga Valley West Shore Model Railroad Club and is now a model train museum. The depot was added to the National Register of Historic Places and is part of the Ohio Historic Inventory.

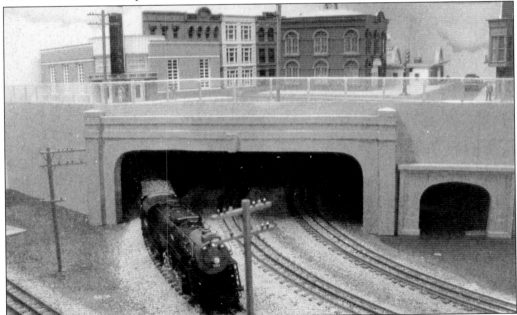

The photograph is of one of the displays in the former depot. The Cuyahoga Valley West Shore Model Railroad Club meets every Thursday at 7:00 p.m. During Heritage Days and other events in the community, the club is open to the public. The depot has been added to the National Register of Historic Places.

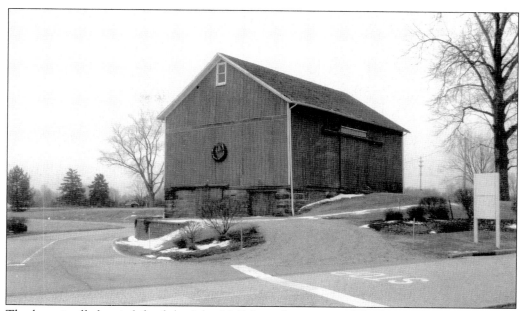

The barn is all that is left of the John Hall farm. It was one of the largest farms of the area. The family home was used for many years as the clubhouse of Home Links Golf Club. The barn, with its extended roof creating a large storage space and a peak projecting above a hayloft opening, is one of the most familiar images associated with prairie barns. John Road is named after John Hall.

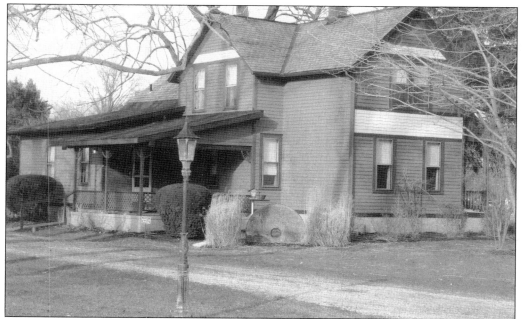

At 23336 West Street, the corner of West Street and Lindberg Boulevard, is the property called Willy Nilly acres. In 1872, John G. Klink purchased 160 acres of land and developed one of the most fertile farms of the area. The farmhouse that stands today replaced the original log and frame house. Today it is a collection of well-preserved farm buildings standing on 13 acres.

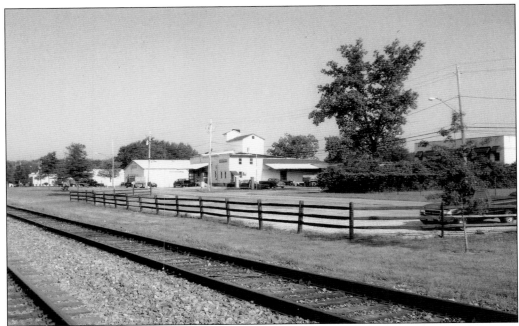

As one looks across the tracks, it can take one back to the 1920s when the United Farmers Exchange was organized. The structure was built as a gristmill for Olmsted Falls Lumber. It was purchased by the United Farmers Exchange and in 1921 moved to its present site. Its stockholders were mostly farmers from Olmsted or the surrounding area. Some of the same people also formed the Ohio Farmers Cooperative Milk Association.

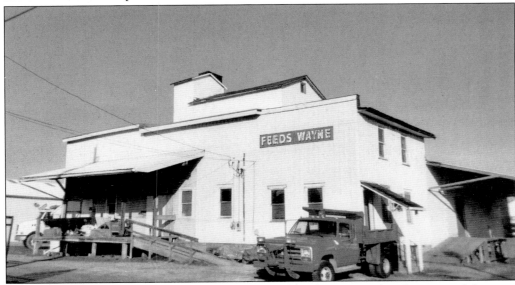

The United Farmers Exchange's building was moved to the site to take advantage of the train depot. Today it is Wayne Feed Store. With a little imagination one can visualize the activity when a train would arrive, the loading and unloading of farm goods to be delivered or taken from the exchange building. The sign of the United Farmers Exchange still exists, though a little rusty.

Four

WESTVIEW

Westview's history coincides with that of Olmsted Falls. The first settler of the area, James Geer, settled in what was then known as Columbia Township in an area that eventually became Westview. Columbia Township was the first township settled west of the Cuyahoga River. Geer blazed trails through the reserve beginning in 1807 and is credited with being the father of the first settler's child born west of the Cuyahoga River. He built a log cabin and set up a tannery and followed a shoemaker trade. He was followed by other New Englanders including Calvin and Lemuel Hoadley, who in 1809 built a saw- and gristmill at the site of what is today the Gibbs Butcher Block. The second Hoadley homestead stood on the site of the clubhouse of the Riverside Golf Club. The homestead was called Westview, and at the time the village was called Hoadley's Mills.

It was in the year of 1849 that the Cleveland, Columbus and Cincinnati Railroad cut through the southeast corner of Olmsted Township. The name Westview was given to the railroad station and then to the township. When the railroad came, it seemed that Westview was destined to become the most important section of the area. The rail station became a very busy place; eight passenger trains made daily stops at the station. The village of Westview grew in the 1870s and 1880s with the arrival of mostly Polish, German, and Irish workers for the railroad, quarries, mills, farms, and later greenhouses.

It was not until 1924 that the Village of Westview was incorporated. In 1954, the Ohio Turnpike came through the village and took over 1,200 acres of former farmland. In 1970, Westview annexed Olmsted Falls.

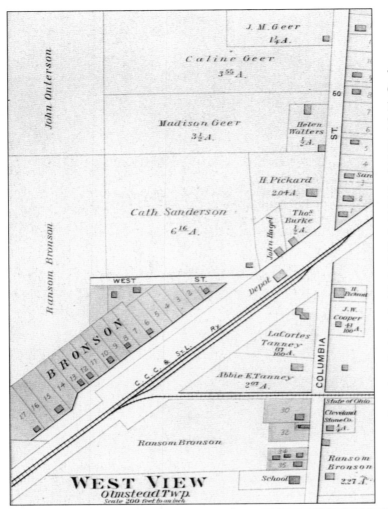

The *Atlas of Cuyahoga County, Ohio* plot plan and business directory identifies "L. C. Tannery, Dealer in Groceries, Drugs, Medicines, Perfumery, Toilet Articles, Books, and Stationery; also, Proprietor of Cheese Factory; capacity 400 cows, or 20 cheeses per day." Today two important business operations still carry the Westview name, West View Lumber and Westview Concrete. It is interesting to note that it seems Westview never decided whether it should be one or two words. The atlas shows it as two words; the *Comprehensive Plan of Westview* completed in the 1960s identifies the name as one word. The photograph below is the business directory as it appears in the atlas.

West View Directory.

L. C. Tanney, Dealer in Groceries, Drugs, Medicines, Perfumery, Toilet Articles, Books, and Stationery; also, Proprietor of Cheese Factory; capacity 400 cows, or 20 cheeses per day.

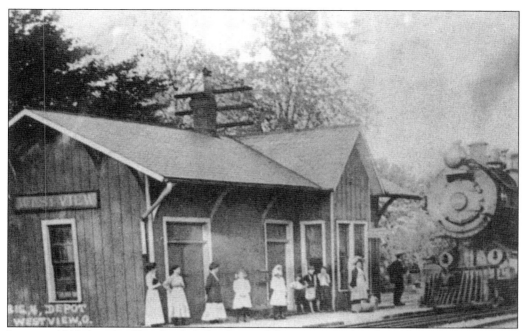

It was in 1849 that the Cleveland, Columbus and Cincinnati Railroad cut through the corner of Olmsted Township at a place that would be called Westview. In 1843, Westview did not exist; it grew because of the railroad. It was reported that Harold Bell Wright, who became a well-known fiction writer, was the telegrapher at the Westview depot for a period of time.

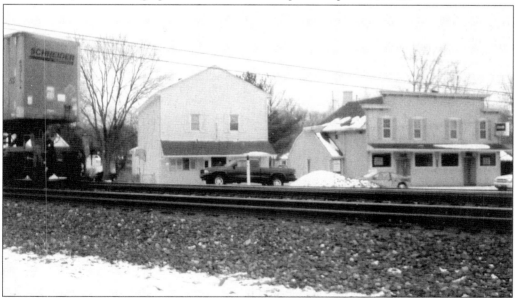

The railroad has not left Westview as the photograph might suggest. It is still a very active railroad crossing, but the train does not stop (at least motorists hope it does not). The buildings that can be seen over the tracks are some of the remaining buildings of the business district of Westview. The Italianate-bracketed building was built in the 1870s in the typical commercial style of the late 19th century.

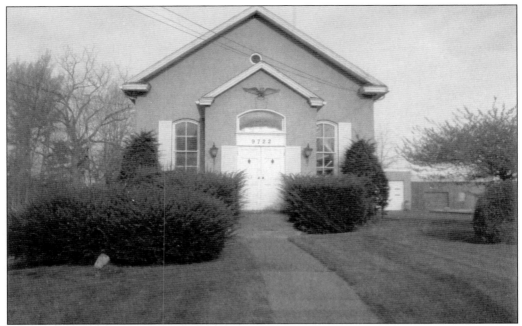

Above is the Westview Town Hall as it appears today. It was built in the 1880s as a schoolhouse and town hall. It was also the center of activity for the community. After annexation, it became Olmsted Falls Town Hall for a period of time.

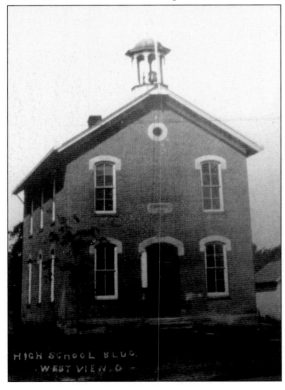

The photograph is from a postcard when the building was the Westview High School and had a second floor. The upper floor was damaged in the windstorm of 1908. When it was rebuilt, it became a one-story building.

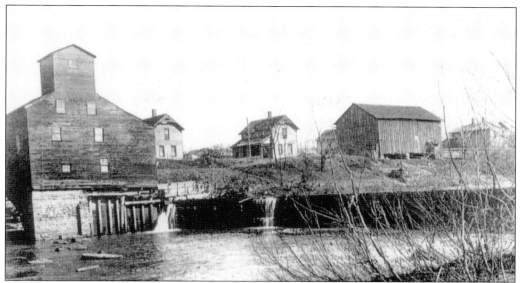

The first major building to be built in what became Westview was the Hoadley Mill. Capt. Calvin Hoadley and his brothers, Lemuel and Samuel, came to Ohio from Watertown, New York, in 1807. The Hoadleys began construction of a sawmill and gristmill that they completed in 1809. This photograph shows the mill when it was in full operation. (Gibbs Butcher Block.)

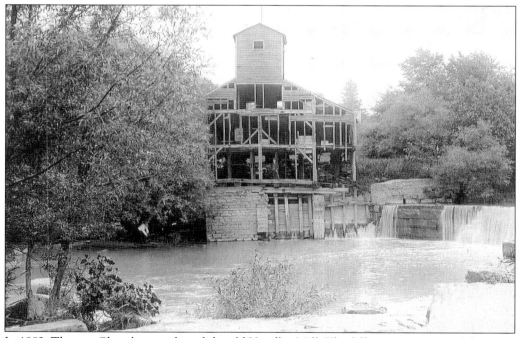

In 1882, Thomas Chamber purchased the old Hoadley Mill. The following year, one of the worst floods in the history of the area nearly tore the mill apart and swept it downstream. He rebuilt the structure, and it was again almost destroyed in the flood of 1913. The mill continued in operation until 1920. This photograph is of the mill as it fell into disrepair. (Bill Nickels collection.)

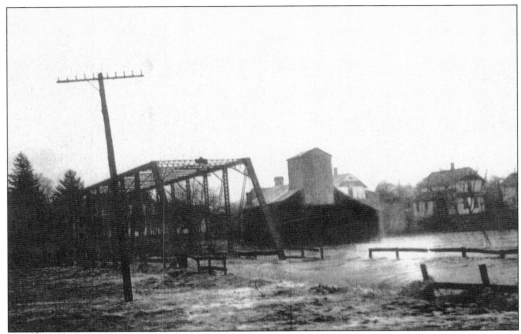

The photograph is of the flood of 1913 that destroyed or severely damaged the mills and bridges along the Rocky River. It was taken at Sprague Road where the bridge and the Hoadley (Chamber) Mill, which were in grave peril, can be seen. (Gibbs Butcher Block.)

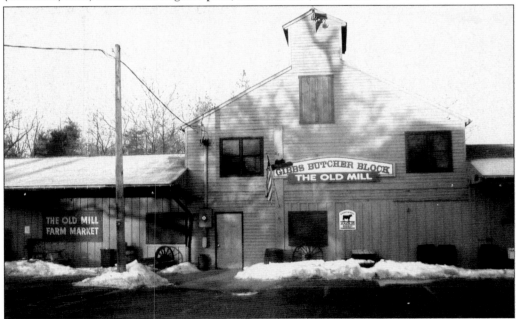

Now on the site of the Hoadley Mill, one will find the Gibbs Butcher Block and the Old Mill Farm Market. It was built to look like the old mill and is located on the same site. Most people who shop here are most likely unaware of the historic significance of the old mill. It was the most important enterprise of Westview.

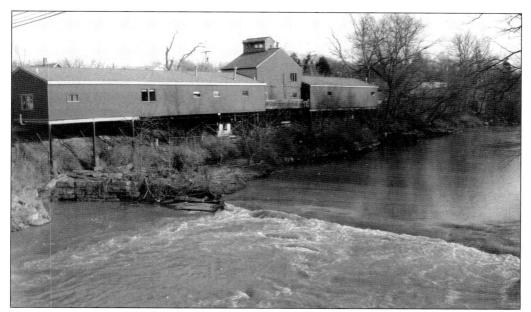

This photograph is of the foundation of the mill today looking across the Rocky River from the Sprague Road Bridge. The back of the Old Mill Farm Market can be seen. In 1882, a man named Thomas Chambers purchased the Hoadley Mill that was built in the 1830s. Floods of 1883 and 1913 practically destroyed the mills of Westview and Olmsted Falls. They were rebuilt, but today only the foundation stones of the great mills can be seen.

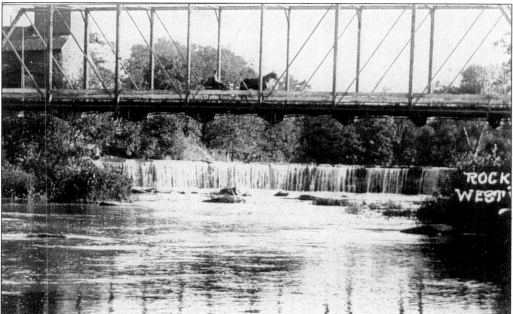

If this photograph of the old Westview Sprague Road Bridge that crossed the Rocky River is looked at closely, a horse and buggy can be seen. The Hoadley home, called Westview, was just across the street from the mill. In the left-hand corner of the photograph the mill can be seen. (Bill Nickels collection.)

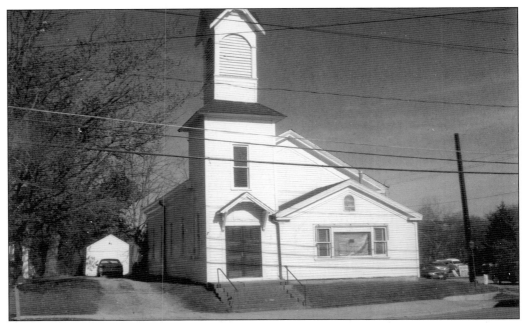

The Geer house (built about 1870) at 9396 Columbia Road is identified as the M. and J. M. Geer house. The Geers had two houses in what was Westview. Even more important than that, it is a remaining structure of the Geer family, recorded as the first settlers of Olmsted in 1814. James Geer has been credited with many antislavery activities as a member of the Wesleyan Methodist church of Westview.

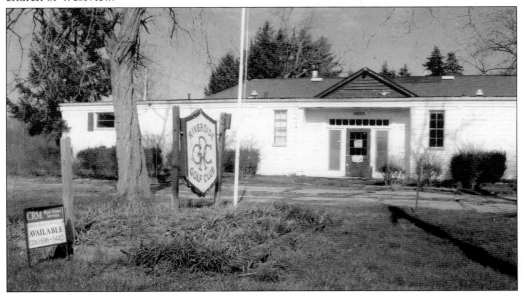

The Wesleyan Methodist church (built about 1845) of Westview today is an antique store. In its day, it was an important institution of Westview. It was built on land deeded to the church by the Hoadley family and affectionately called Hoadley Mill Church. The Wesleyan Methodists were followers of John Wesley, an 18th-century Anglican evangelist and founder of the Wesleyan tradition. For many years it served as an antique store.

Five

SCHOOLS

The first schools of the Western Reserve were most often started in the cabins of early settlers, then in religious institutions supported by contributions of local residents. In 1821, the state legislature authorized villages and townships to establish public schools by levying taxes, but it was not a mandatory order.

In Olmsted Township the first school was located near the Hoadley Mill on Calvin Geer's farm in the 1840s, in what became the village of Westview. The village green schoolhouse pavilion marks the location of the first frame school in Olmsted Falls that was replaced by a redbrick schoolhouse. The Union Schoolhouse, or what was more affectionately called "the Big Little Red Schoolhouse," built in 1874, served until 1914 when it was declared unsafe. Classes were held in the Olmsted Falls community building until the Olmsted Falls Village School was opened in 1916. It serves today as city hall and police headquarters.

Today Olmsted Falls's schools pride themselves on outstanding academic programs, modern facilities, and a dedicated staff. Olmsted Falls's city school district is comprised of Falls-Lenox Primary School, Fitch Intermediate School, Olmsted Falls Middle School, and Olmsted Falls High School. A seven-room addition was built onto the elementary section of the high school building in 1948. When that proved inadequate in the late 1950s, the Lenox Primary School was built in 1960 on the 19 acres of land abutting the high school. Olmsted Falls schools have achieved Ohio's highest academic ranking for six consecutive years, and more than 25 students have qualified as national merit scholars in the last six years. The Falls-Lenox Primary School had the distinction of being selected as an Ohio Hall of Fame school. St. Mary of the Falls Catholic School on Columbia and Bagley Roads conducts classes from grades prekindergarten through eighth grade with an enrollment of 267 students. Olmsted Falls Community Church, of 7853 Main Street, has a preschool program and provides Christian education classes for ages three years through the seventh grade every Sunday morning.

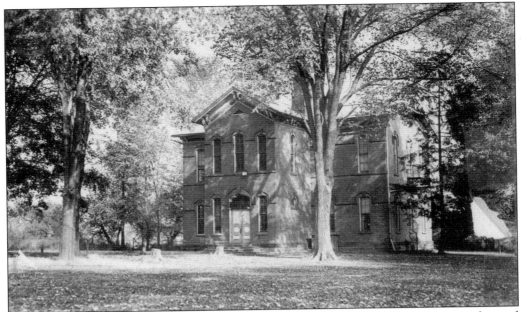

Pictured is the brick schoolhouse that stood at the rear of the village green on property donated to the community by the Barnum family. Built in 1874, the school had three departments: primary, intermediate, and high school. It was hailed as a great step forward in education. When a new school was built in 1916, it became the town hall. It also served as a meeting hall for the Boy Scouts, the Masonic Lodge, and Eastern Star. It was torn down in 1960.

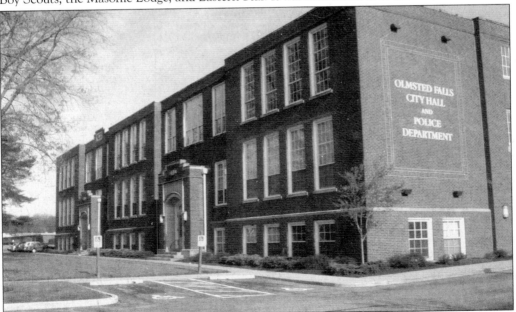

The Olmsted Falls primary and high school was built in 1916 with additions added over the years. Today it serves as city hall and police headquarters. On May 26, 1967, Dr. Donald Cobb, superintendent of schools, broke ground for Olmsted Falls's new high school that is located at 26939 Bagley Road.

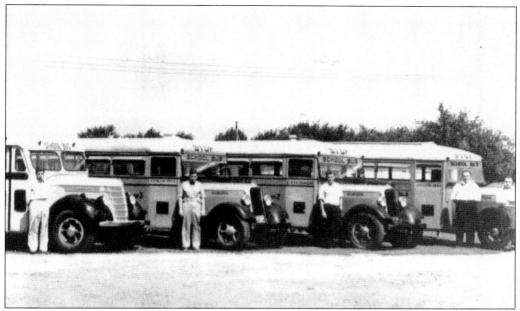

The first large schoolhouse west of the Rocky River was at Ridgeville, an adjoining township, so transportation was a problem. At first horse-drawn wagons were used. Gradually wagons were replaced by farm trucks that were covered with a tarpaulin stretched over the carriage of the truck as a tent with a rear gate and steps. Later regular bus service was contracted to successful bidders who owned and operated their own buses. The proud owners are pictured above.

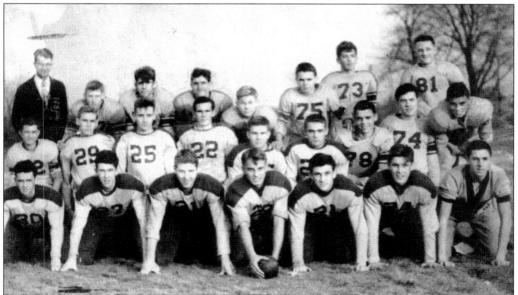

The 1959 Olmsted Falls Bulldogs football team became the undefeated champions of the Southwest District Class A division. After the school left the one-room schoolhouse, sports became an important part of school programs. Football always seemed to have the largest following, and Olmsted Falls has produced some great football teams. (Cleveland State University, Cleveland Press Collection.)

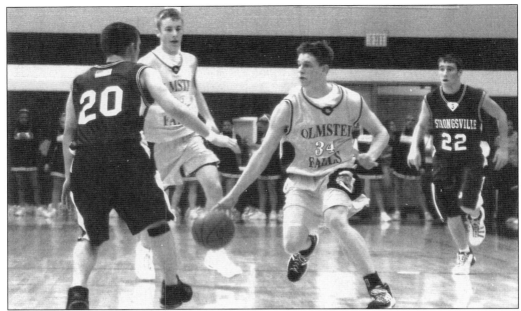

Basketball has continued to be an important part of the Olmsted Falls sports program. Head coach Pat Donahue took the boys' basketball team to an 18-2 record during the regular season in 2007. It had a great year with the starting lineup of Tyler Sparks, Dave and Pat Pellerite, and seniors Alex Sedley and Mike Stallard. (Madere's SpectraLight Photography and Design.)

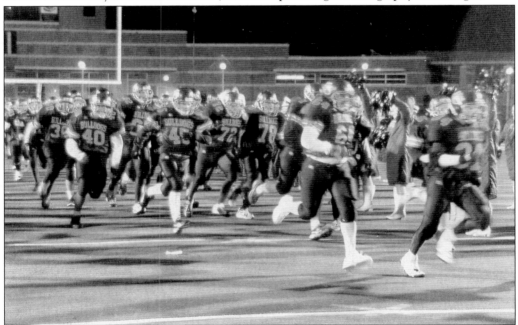

As early as 1921, Olmsted Falls had a football team, and in the years of 1959 and 2000, it became division and state champions. As one enters Olmsted Falls, one is reminded that it is the home of the Division 2 football state champions of 2000, taken there by coach Jim Ryan and his staff. (Madere's SpectraLight Photography and Design.)

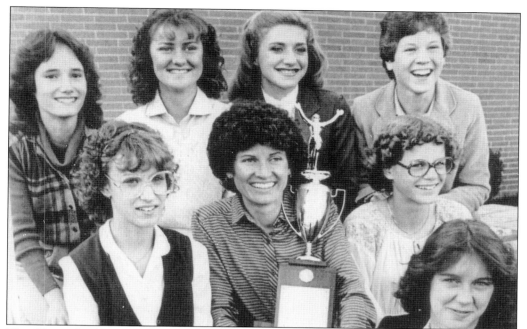

The Olmsted Falls state cross-country championship team is seen here. They are, from left to right, (first row) Lisa DeWillie; (second row) Laura Bennell, coach Rae Alexander, and Michelle Kalikin; (third row) Kathy Vrry, Lisa Moore, Debbie Lloyd, and Gretchen Chubb. (Cleveland State University, Cleveland Press Collection.)

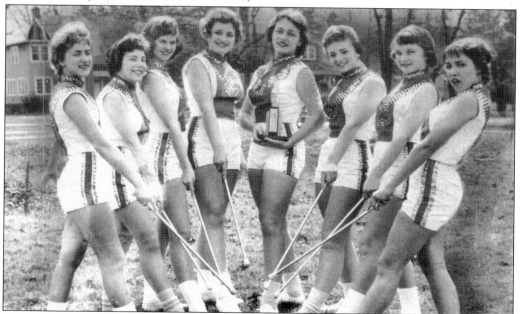

The 1959 twirling champions of Olmsted Falls High School are seen here. The girls won the first-place trophy in competition with other high school majorettes. They are, from left to right, Sharon Martell, Sharon Tober, Joan Oring, Marcia Watson, Sally Stark, Jeannie Venefra, Linda Lamb, and Beverly Dill. (Cleveland State University, Cleveland Press Collection.)

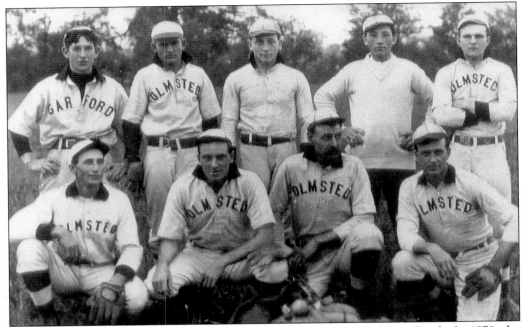

As early as 1876, a baseball team was organized in the village called Ever Ready. In 1878, the team was called the Broom Makers. They played teams from throughout the area. In 1904, the Olmsted Athletic Club defeated a team from as far away as central Africa. Olmsted Falls won the Cuyahoga County baseball championship in 1930. (Cleveland State University, Cleveland Press Collection.)

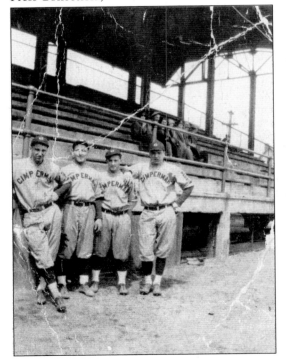

This was the author's grandfather's Class A team that was called Cimperman Coal on which both his father and uncle played. The author's father would tell him about how teams from Cleveland would travel around the county playing games in the small towns, one of which was Olmsted Falls. The photograph to the left is when they won the league championship and played at historic League Park in Cleveland. They are, from left to right, Anthony Cimperman, John Lock, Steve Metro, and John Cimperman.

Six

Grand Pacific Junction

The site of Grand Pacific Junction was the town center of Olmsted Falls. By the 1970s, the buildings within Grand Pacific Junction had fallen into disrepair, but they remained intact. Interest in the preservation of the buildings began in the mid-1970s when the Grand Pacific Hotel was placed on the National Register of Historic Places of the National Park Service. But it was not until 1989 that Clint Williams, a longtime Olmsted Falls resident and successful real estate entrepreneur, purchased the entire site with the intent of restoring the buildings and returning the area into the bustling commercial district that it is today.

A wonderful walk through the district should begin at the Grand Pacific Hotel, the oldest commercial structure in Grand Pacific Junction. It was constructed sometime between the 1830s or 1840s as a seminary school located on Lewis Road. It must have been quite a feat to move that large building to its present location in 1858. When it opened as a hotel, it became the social center of the Olmsted Falls community. Its name changed over the years: in 1872 as Olmsted Falls Hotel; in 1874 as De-Carpenter Hotel; then in 1877 as the Dougherty Hotel; and in 1893, it became the Peltz and Simmerer Hardware Store. In 1904, the second floor became a dentist office. In 1912, a drugstore was opened in the building. Over the years the building had many uses, but the hardware store continued in the building until the store closed in the mid-1970s. As of 2007, it is again called the Grand Pacific Hotel and serves as a banquet facility. The building is listed on the National Register of Historic Places of the National Park Service.

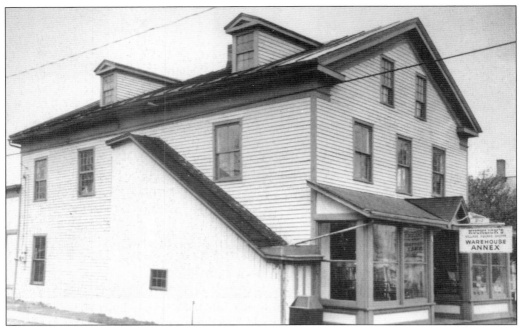

This photograph shows the Grand Pacific Hotel when it did not look so grand before restoration. The years as a hardware store and warehouse for the hardware store took its toll. It was not until the mid-1970s that the store closed. The building is considered the oldest commercial building in Olmsted Falls.

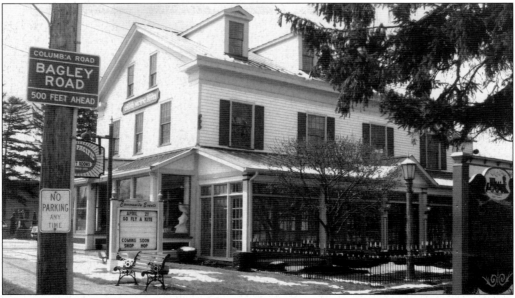

The Grand Pacific Hotel at 8112 Columbia Road is seen as it appears today as a banquet facility. The building is listed on National Register of Historic Places and was built about 1840 as a seminary school. It was moved to its present location from Lewis Road in 1858 and opened as the Grand Pacific Hotel. As a hotel it had a tragic beginning. Thomas Brown, the first proprietor of the hotel, was murdered on his way to a bank in Cleveland.

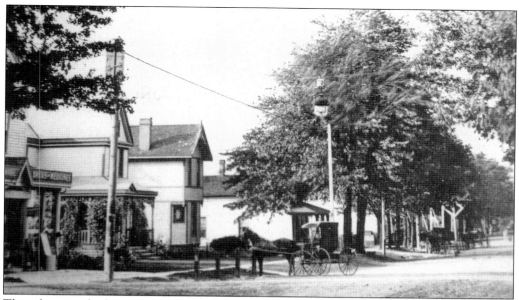

This photograph shows the business district in the late 1800s. If one looks above the horse and buggy, one can see an arc lamp that would have been in front of Simmerer Hardware Store, today's Grand Pacific Hotel. The photograph includes the buildings on the west side of Columbia Road, which are, from left to right, Simmerer Hardware Store and the Joseph Peltz and Philip Simmerer home.

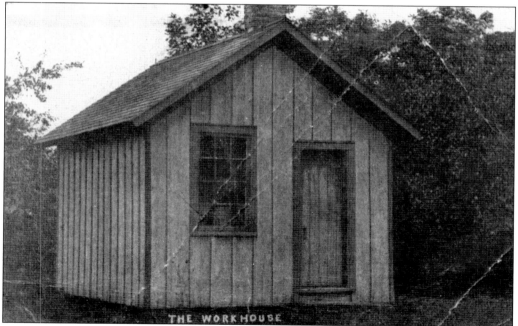

THE WORKHOUSE

A postcard of the Olmsted Falls jail called it the "workhouse." It may be hard to envision doing much work in the 10-by-20-foot building. The postcard dates from a time when it could be mailed for 1¢. The jail is now part of Grand Pacific Junction as can be seen from the following picture. (Ann Marie Donegan collection.)

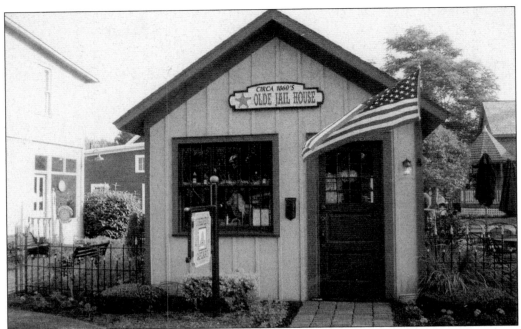

The Olde Jail House (built about 1860) was moved to 25546 Mill Street in 1924. It was only used to keep prisoners overnight for a minor offense. For more serious crimes, they were taken to jails in other communities. After 1924, prisoners were locked up in two jail cells in the closed Union Schoolhouse on the village green. The Olde Jail House is now a gift shop.

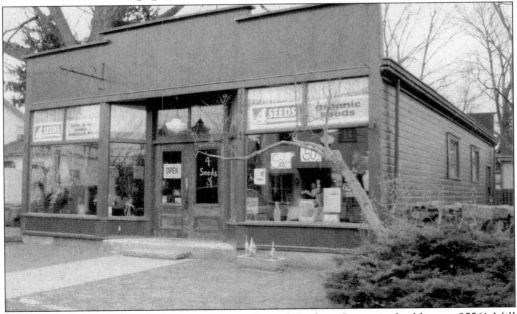

Just across Mill Street is the 4 Seeds Mercantile and Trading Company building at 25561 Mill Street. Today it is an organic food and gift shop, but over the years, it served the community with many uses during its changing times. The building was built about 1909 by James Burns as a Ford and Willis Knight automobile dealership showroom.

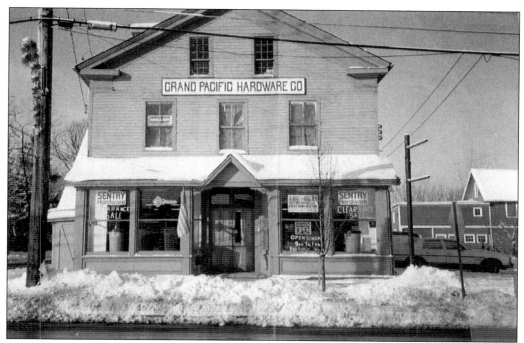

Olmsted Falls in the days of the horse and buggy was just an outlining settlement of Cleveland. Cleveland had already developed into a commercial center where most of the wearing apparel, hardware, foodstuff, and other goods could be obtained.

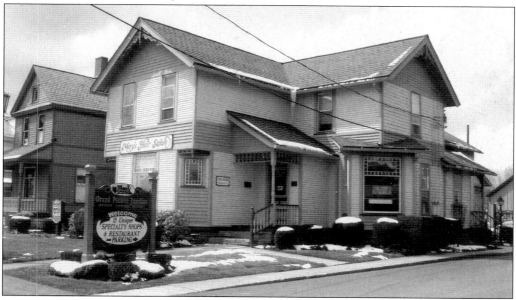

It was in 1881 that Peltz, known as Joe, married Anna Simmerer. In 1882, he opened a drug and hardware store and later opened a soda fountain in the same building. In 1888, he and his brother-in-law Philip Simmerer became partners in the Peltz and Simmerer Hardware Store. The photograph above is of the Peltz homestead that is located at 8086 Columbia Road. The home now serves as Mary's Hair Salon.

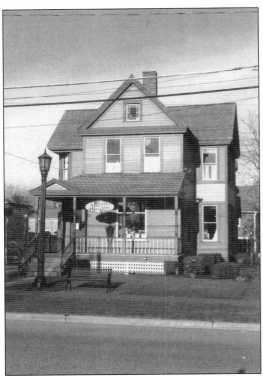

Philip Simmerer built his home (about 1897) at 8096 Columbia Road. Simmerer was one of the founding partners of the Peltz and Simmerer Hardware Store. Simmerer and his wife, Margaret, came to Olmsted Falls in 1886. The family was always considered influential in community affairs. Walter F. Holzworth, in his book *Historical Story Olmsted Township*, calls Simmerer and his family "one of Olmsted Falls great institutions."

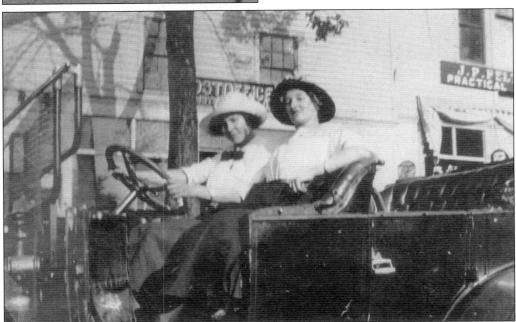

This photograph was taken in front of the Peltz Hardware Store, today's Grand Pacific Hotel, in 1913. The car was owned by realtor Frank Bodecker. It is believed that the ladies are Mrs. Bodecker and her daughter. At that time, if one was going to show something off it would be in front of the Peltz Hardware Store.

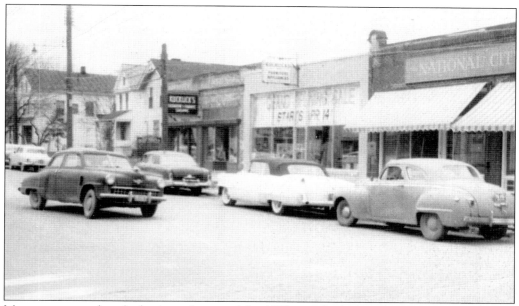

Many can remember the business district of the 1950s as it looked in the photograph. It is now called Grand Pacific Junction and a great deal more attractive and representative of the area as it was in the late 1880s.

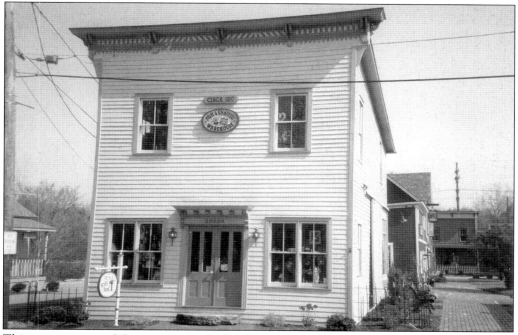

This two-story wood frame commercial building was used for many years as a warehouse for the Peltz and Simmerer Hardware Store. Built in the Italianate style about 1870, its bracketed cornice forms a parapet to the sloping shed roof. Prior to the development of Grand Pacific Junction, it served as an antique shop called the Green Barn Shop. Today it is a day spa called A Time to Spa.

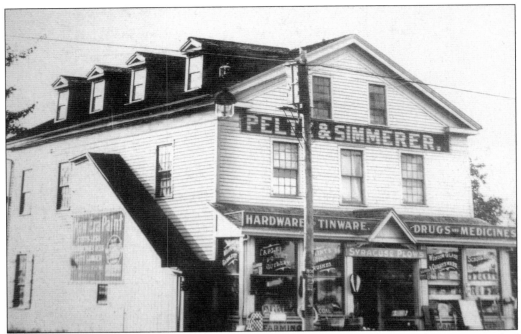

This photograph, taken in front of the Peltz and Simmerer Hardware Store, is from a postcard of Olmsted Falls. It was in 1893 that Joseph Peltz and his brother-in-law Philip Simmerer opened a hardware, drug, and general store in the former Dougherty Hotel, today's Grand Pacific Hotel.

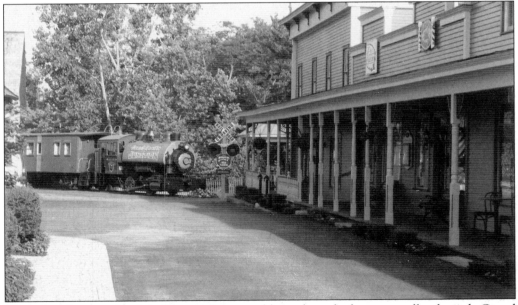

The grand history of railroading can be seen, felt, and touched as one walks through Grand Pacific Junction. This 1927 Vulcan steam engine No. 100 and caboose are on display overlooking Plum Creek. A few steps away is the boardwalk of Grand Pacific Junction where one can find Northrop Bookstore, the Bead Shop, Depot Barber Shop, and the Falls Crossing Restaurant, Bar, and Party Room.

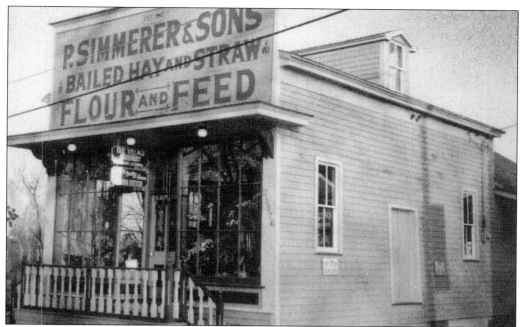

If it was not in the hardware store, it might be found in the feed store. Called the granary (built about 1900), this post and beam construction building served as a grain, flour, and feed store. The original grain bins are still intact on the second floor. Hay was also stored above drop-through trapdoors to the first-floor loading platforms.

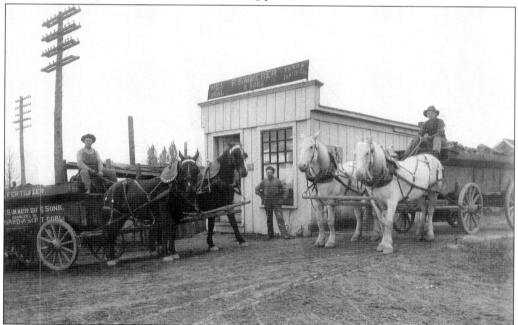

Even the feed store grew. Simmerer and Sons did not miss much. According to the signage on the wagon, it delivered coal as well as fertilizer, hopefully not on the same wagon. Philip Simmerer and his family operated a hardware and farm supply business in the village for 78 years.

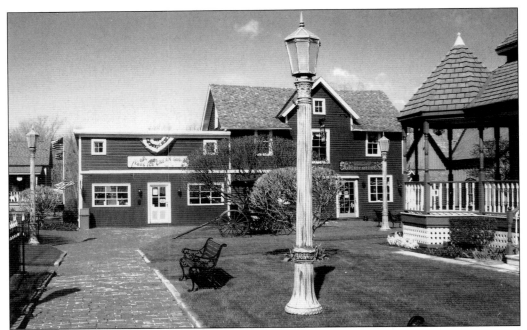

The livery stable was built about 1898 for the Grand Pacific Hotel for hotel guests. It was later used by the Peltz and Simmer Hardware Store as a stable and storage shed. Today it is an ice-cream parlor and the very popular Clementine's Restaurant.

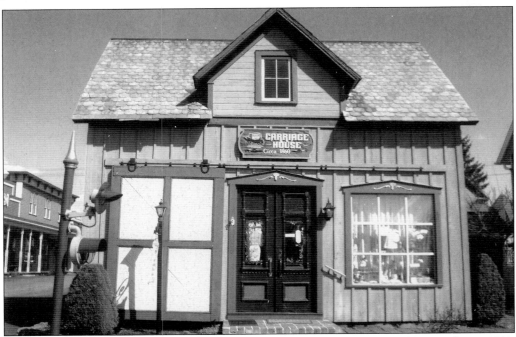

The carriage house was built in the 1860s to serve its main house that was lost in a fire in 1912. The carriage house was located next to the Peltz homestead. After the fire, it was moved to its present location and used by Kucklick's Village Square Shoppe as a storage barn.

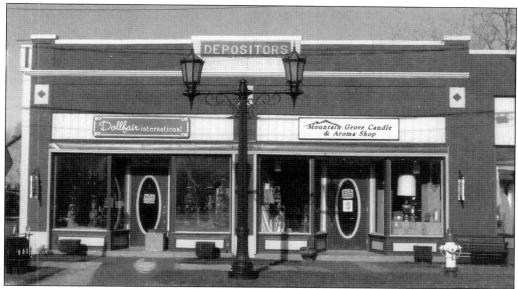

Depositor's Bank, like many other banks throughout the country, failed in the Wall Street crash of 1929. The bank had only been in business for five years before the collapse of the stock market. Most people have heard about the business crash of 1929, but not many Americans know of the crash of 1937. Practically all the banks of Cuyahoga County closed during that eight-year period.

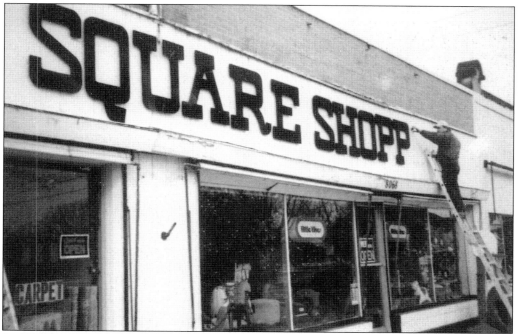

In 1940, Fritz Kucklick and his son moved their appliance and furniture store into the defunct Depositor's Bank building. It was later named Kucklick's Village Square Shoppe. That store closed in 1990. The building is now occupied by Dollfair International and Mountain Grove Candle Aroma Shop. Next door is Julianne's Bridal Outlet and Resale Shop.

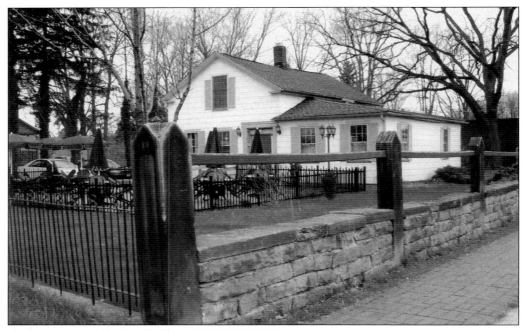

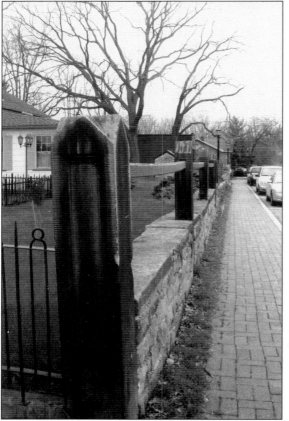

No. 8134 Columbia Road (built about 1840), known in the early days of the community as the Waring estate, was built by William Waring. The Warings sold the building to Sylvester Alcott who, along with his brother Levi, started a sawmill on Plum Creek that was the forerunner of the Alcott and Stokes Mill. It also was the home of James Burns, and all of the owners had an impact on the history of Olmsted Falls. Burns built his automobile dealership on the property. The patterned wrought iron fence and sandstone carved gabled posts that surround the home have been preserved over the years and hopefully for many more years to come. Today the building is the popular Bistro Du Beaujolais Restaurant.

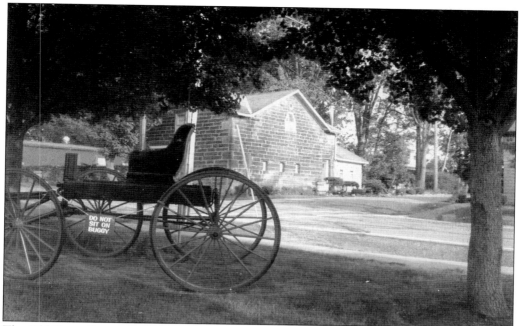

The Old Stone Barn at 8136 Mill Street (built about 1854) and the livery stable were built by Waring as a stable and blacksmith shop. In 1909, a man named Burns bought the property and used the barn as a stable and built an automobile dealership between the home and livery stable. It is now a private residence.

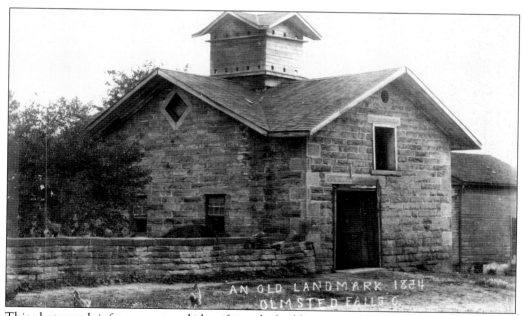

This photograph is from a postcard identifying the building as an old landmark of Olmsted Falls. It is evident that there was a frame addition or building next to it when the stone building was used as a barn and stable. It also had quite a birdhouse on its roof.

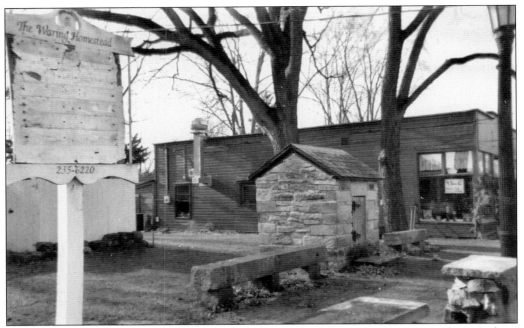

This sandstone icehouse that was part of the Waring-Alcott House is on its original site. It dates from a time when there were no refrigerators. If people could afford it, they may also have had an icebox in the home.

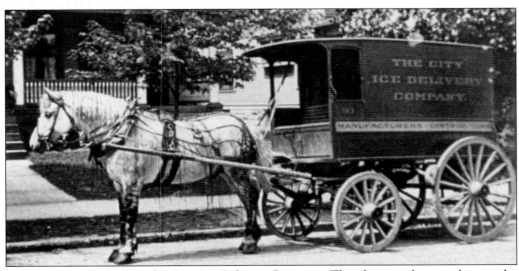

This ice wagon was from the City Ice Delivery Company. The photograph was taken in the 1920s. One of the early ice companies was the Kelly Brothers, which would bring the ice that was cut from Lake Erie near Kelly's Island to Cleveland and its suburban locations.

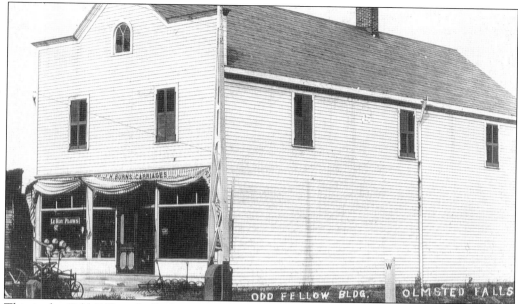

This is the Odd Fellows hall when it stood at 8017 Columbia Road. If one looks closely at the awning, J. H. Burns Carriages can be seen. In 1896, Burns took over the farm implement and carriage business of his stepfather, James Hendrickson, the village blacksmith. Around 1900, Henry Fenderbosch became Burns's partner. The building was moved when the railroad tracks were expanded to a four-track system.

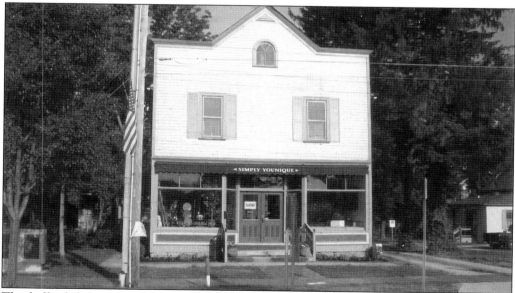

The hall of the Odd Fellows, a fraternal organization formed for social and entertainment activities, was located at 8154 Columbia Road. Their building was originally located at 8017 Columbia Road, the site of the Falls Veterinary Clinic parking lot today. The original building was destroyed by fire in 1903 and rebuilt at the same location. The building became known as Grange Hall and continued under that use until 2003. The building is now used as a specialty shop.

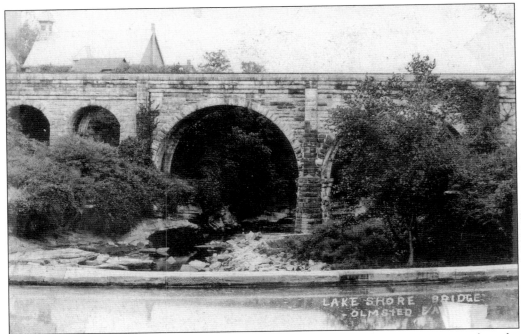

The 1909 railroad bridge was built to accommodate a four-track rail system at a time when the railroad traffic was continuing to grow. The construction of the bridge caused the move of the Odd Fellows hall to its present location. This massive, broad concrete arch span replaced an earlier stone arched bridge, seen above. (Bill Nickels collection.)

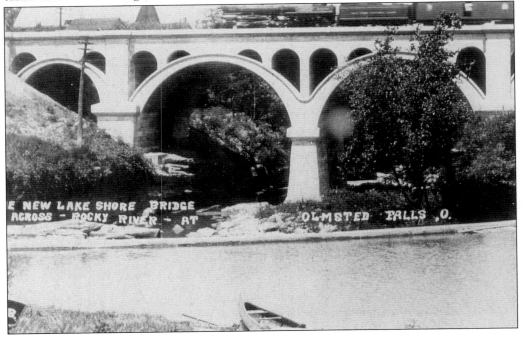

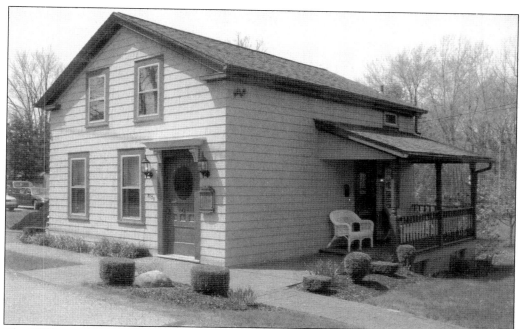

The William TeGrotenhuis home (built about 1860), located at 8130 Orchard Road, is one of the better-preserved Greek Revival–style cottages in the Olmsted Falls business district. It is interesting to note that the name TeGrotenhuis in Dutch means "big house." The family eventually purchased one of the largest homes in Olmsted Falls.

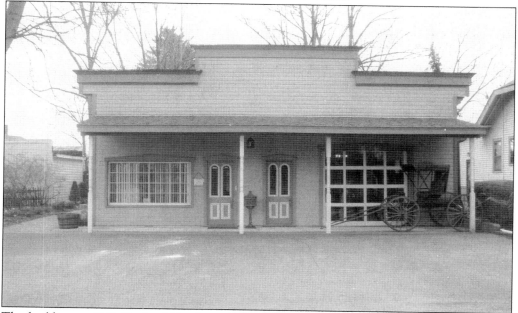

The building at 8153 Orchard Road was built in the 1940s as the Willis Knight service and repair garage. The automobile garage served the needs of many a needy motorist of the Olmsted Falls area. Today it is the home of Evergreen Title Agency. In the picture window of the title agency is a carriage with mannequins that takes viewers back to a time before the automobile.

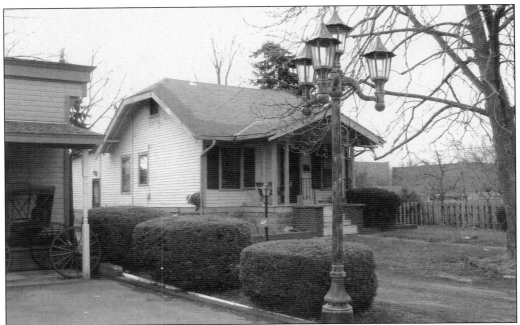

This photograph is of a Sears catalog house with a street address of 8161 Orchard Street. It is the model known as the Rodessa. The Sears catalog reads, "The Rodessa provides real low-cost comfort and fine appearance. The house is simple and inexpensive to build and requires only a 28-foot lot. The Rodessa proved to be one of our most popular catalog houses." In the 1933 catalog, the price was $931.

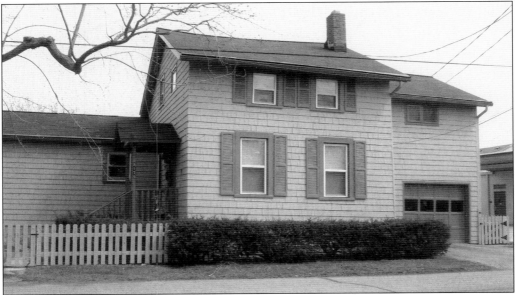

The house at 8179 Orchard Street (built about 1870) is included on the Ohio Historic Inventory as one of the older houses of the area that represents an example of a late-19th-century vernacular architecture in Olmsted Falls. Although the house has undergone alterations, it retains its basic historic character.

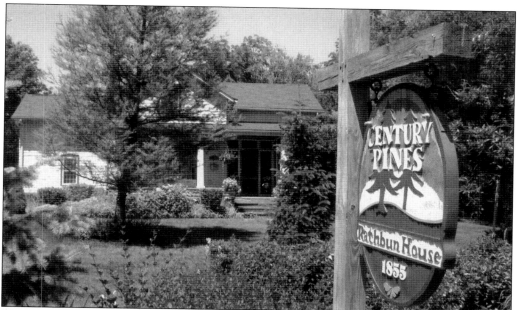

The Rathbun House at 25746 Bagley Road (built about 1855) is called Century Pines. In 1883, Charles Rathbun invented a device for sewing leather. He called the invention the Leather Edge Meeting Machine. Aschel Osborn and Rathbun had a well-drilling business. They set up a steam-driven apparatus to replace the horse sweep in drilling for oil. The great wealth from oil never came, but Rathbun had other talents as a cartoonist and artist.

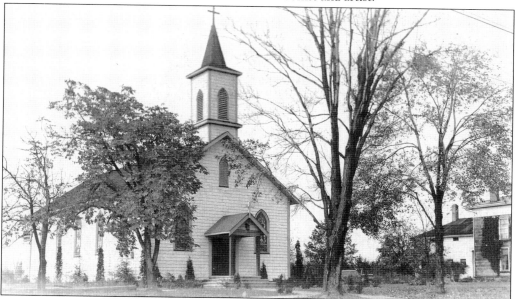

As one leaves Grand Pacific Junction, St. Mary of the Falls Catholic Church can be seen. In 1856, Fr. Louis J. Filliere, the first resident pastor, built a small wooden church on what is today the parking lot of the Olmsted Community Church. In 1873, Father Filliere purchased the property on the southwest corner of Hamlin (Bagley) and Columbia Roads. The church was then moved to that location and enlarged.

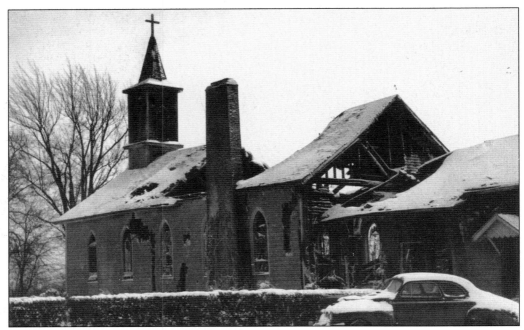

The St. Mary of the Falls Catholic Church disastrous fire of 1948 left the Catholics of Olmsted without a church, but almost immediately on September 5, 1948, ground was broken for a new church. On May 20, 1950, the magnificent new church was dedicated. (Michelle Neudeck collection.)

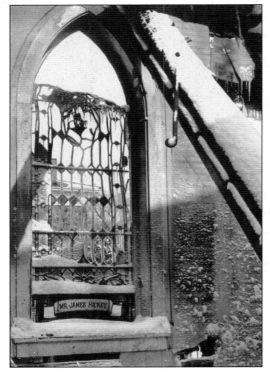

This leaded stained-glass window was dedicated to the Hickey family. James Hickey is credited with being the second Catholic to settle in Olmsted Falls; the first was John Reynolds. The Hickey home served as St. Mary of the Falls Catholic Church from 1851 to 1854. Because the priest had to come from Elyria, a mass was said once every other month. (Michelle Neudeck collection.)

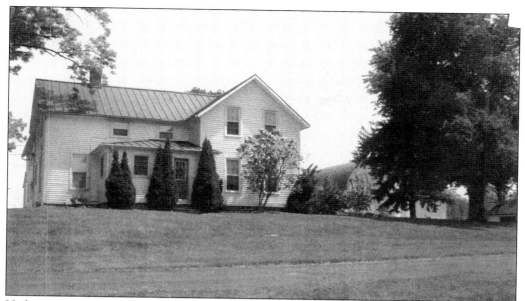

Hickey came to Olmsted Falls in 1849. In 1850, he married Mary Fitch. Hickey became a very prominent farmer and landowner and also served as a township trustee. He started as a stonemason then worked as a bridge builder. He was in charge of the construction of the Cleveland, Columbus, and Cincinnati Railroad bridge over the Rocky River in Westview in 1849. He owned much of the property that is now Bagley Road, and this is one of the reasons it was called Irish Road before being renamed Bagley Road.

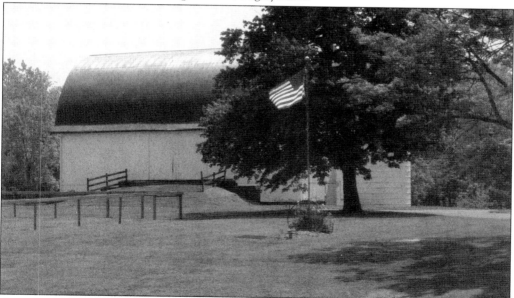

As early as 1860, Hickey began to invest his earnings in farmland and became one of the largest landowners in the area. At one time, he owned over 1,000 acres. The magnificent barn was built in the prairie style to accommodate large herds of livestock and storage space needed for hay and feed. The extended roof creates the large storage space. In 1942, the Methodist Children's Home purchased the Hickey farm.

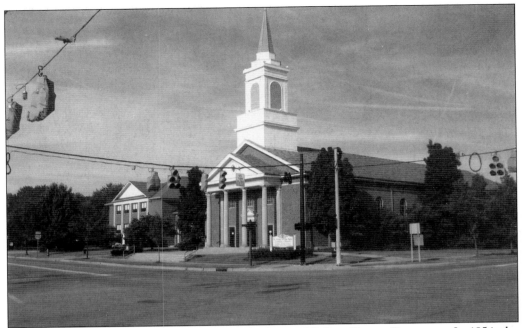

The first Catholic mass was held in 1849 in the barn of Calvin Geer, a Protestant. In 1854, the parishioners of St. Mary of the Falls Catholic Church gathered for mass on Sundays in the log schoolhouse on the village green, establishing the founding of the parish. The church Web page states, "The United States was barely 78 years old, Franklin Pierce was President and the Civil War was yet to be fought." The photograph is of St. Mary of the Falls Catholic Church today.

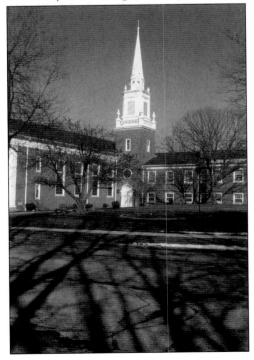

The tall and illuminated spires of St. Mary of the Falls Catholic Church and Olmsted Community Church, at either end of the Olmsted Falls business district, provide magnificent landmarks for ground and air travelers alike. Today St. Mary of the Falls Catholic Church serves more than 2,300 families in faith and has a school with an enrollment of more than 260 students from prekindergarten through the eighth grade. The pastor is Fr. Robert Cole.

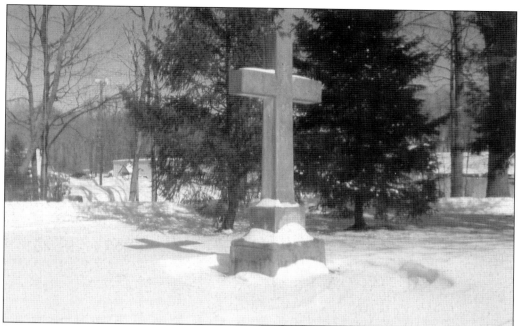

St. Mary of the Falls Cemetery was opened in 1874 when Bishop Gilmore of the Diocese of Cleveland purchased land along what was then called Irish Road and Dutch Road (its first name was Hamlin Road, now Bagley Road). Walking through a cemetery, much of the history of a community can be learned; the headstones and monuments continue to record that ongoing story of life.

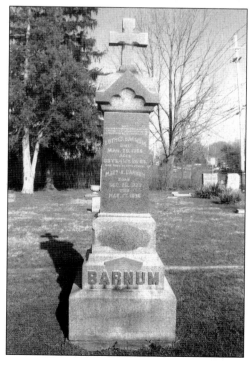

Luther Barnum, of quarry and community fame, married Anna Reynolds, a daughter of John Reynolds, who was one of the first Catholics to settle in Olmsted. Barnum became a Catholic and his wife, family, and descendants were devoted and active members of the churches of St. Mary of the Falls of Olmsted Falls and St. Mary's of Berea.

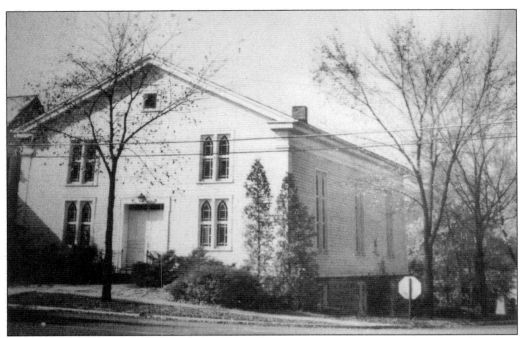

The bell tower that was lost in a windstorm in 1908 was rebuilt. It now serves as the Grand Pacific Wedding Chapel. It is a nondenominational chapel. The photograph is of the chapel before restoration.

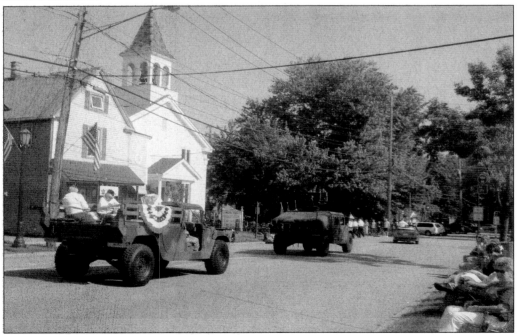

The building is seen in this image after restoration, with its rebuilt bell tower that embellishes its presence in the historic central business district of Olmsted Falls. The photograph was taken during the 2007 Memorial Day parade.

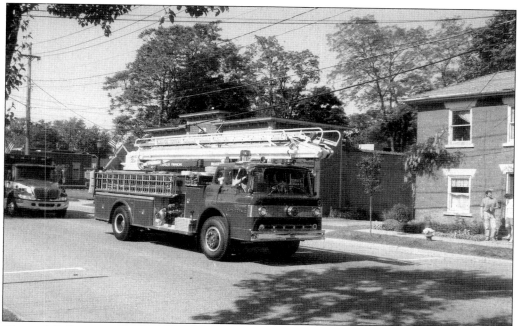

Olmsted Falls is proud of its police and fire departments. Its modern fire truck in the 2007 Memorial Day parade provides assurance to adults and a thrill to the young.

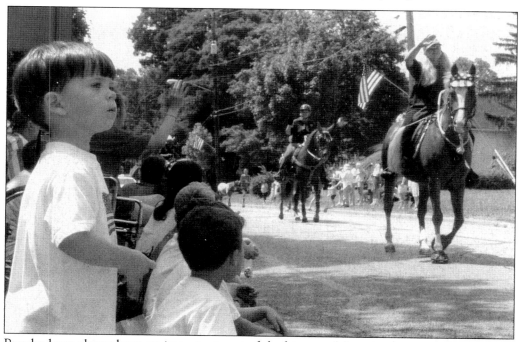

Parades have always been an important part of the history of American cities and towns, and Olmsted Falls is no exception. They bring people together and provide entertainment for the young and old. A parade gives a community an opportunity to celebrate its past and exhibit its progress. (Madere's SpectraLight Photography and Designs.)

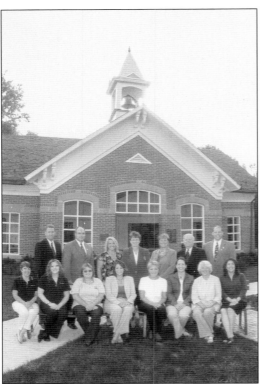

Olmsted Falls has an active chamber of commerce. The photograph to the left of the members was taken on the village green in front of the Red Brick School House Pavilion. The pavilion was build to remind people of the important part the Red Brick School House played in the history of Olmsted Falls. (Madere's SpectraLight Photography and Design).

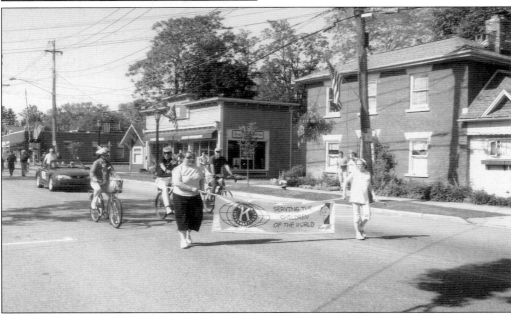

The Kiwanis Club of Olmsted Falls was founded in 1927. The club began with just 35 members and has grown to its current 2007 membership of 79. The first president was Charles H. Lee, and the first secretary was Charles J. Bonsey, who held the post for 17 years. The photograph is of the Kiwanis Club banner in the Memorial Day parade.

BIBLIOGRAPHY

Early Settlers Association Board of Trustees. *Annals of the Early Settlers Association of the Western Reserve, 1983–2003*. Cleveland: West Press Printing, 2003.

Eiben, Christopher J. *Henry B. Payne and Cleveland's First Railroad*. 2005.

Franklin, Nancy L. *Olmsted Falls, Ohio: Walking Through History: A Self-Guided Tour.* OH: 2004.

Frostville. Olmsted Falls, OH: Olmsted Historical Society, 2007.

Holzworth, Walter F. *Historical Story Olmsted Township, Villages of Olmsted Falls, North Olmsted.* West View, OH: 1966.

———. *Story of Cedar Point Valley*. 1980.

Marshall, Sir Knight George L., Jr. "Chief Joseph Brant." *Knight Templar Magazine* XXIII, no. 11 (November 1977).

Offenberg, Bernice (Weitzel). *Over the Years in Olmsted, Township 6, Range 15*. Olmsted Falls, OH: 1969.

Olmsted Falls Homecoming Souvenir Program. Olmsted Falls, OH: Olmsted Falls Homecoming Association, 1939.

Rose, William Ganson. *Cleveland, the Making of a City*. Cleveland: The World Publishing Company, 1950.

Upton, Harriet Taylor. *History of the Western Reserve*. Chicago: Lewis Publishing Company, 1910.

Van Tassel, David D., and John J. Grabowski, eds. *The Encyclopedia of Cleveland History*. Bloomington: Indiana University Press, 1987.

ACROSS AMERICA, PEOPLE ARE DISCOVERING SOMETHING WONDERFUL. *THEIR HERITAGE.*

Arcadia Publishing is the leading local history publisher in the United States. With more than 3,000 titles in print and hundreds of new titles released every year, Arcadia has extensive specialized experience chronicling the history of communities and celebrating America's hidden stories, bringing to life the people, places, and events from the past. To discover the history of other communities across the nation, please visit:

www.arcadiapublishing.com

Customized search tools allow you to find regional history books about the town where you grew up, the cities where your friends and family live, the town where your parents met, or even that retirement spot you've been dreaming about.

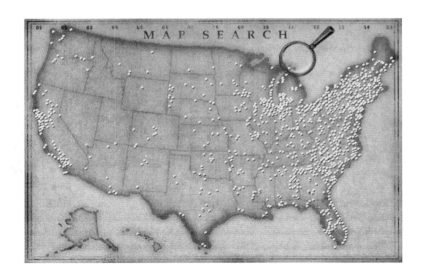